Introduction

John Webster (c1580-c1634)

Although John Webster's writing career is fairly well documented, there is little factual evidence about his life. Probably born in London no later than 1580, Webster was the son of a coach maker and hirer. He may have been educated at the Merchant Taylors' school and probably studied law at the Middle Temple. His relatively meagre output suggests that he may not have been a full-time writer. In 1602 the theatrical entrepreneur Philip Henslowe paid him for contributions to several plays co-written with other writers including Michael Drayton, Thomas Middleton, and Thomas Heywood. In 1604-5 he was involved in the so-called war of the theatres (between the fashionable children's companies and the adult companies) as collaborator with Thomas Dekker on *Westward Ho* and *Northward Ho*. *The White Devil* was staged unsuccessfully at the Red Bull theatre in 1612 and *The Duchess of Malfi* successfully at the Blackfriars theatre in 1613-4. Despite this early flurry of activity, Webster appears to have been a slow writer: in the Preface to *The White Devil* he says 'I do not write with a goose-quill winged with two feathers', and he was described in 1617 as a 'crabbed ... playwright-cartwright'. He wrote some verse, a Lord Mayor's Pageant, a number of other plays, some independently, some collaboratively, and was, presumably, dead by 1634 when Heywood referred to him in the past tense.

What Happens in the Play

The widowed Duchess of Malfi secretly marries her steward Antonio, despite the opposition of her brothers, Duke Ferdinand and the Cardinal, to the idea of her remarrying. Bosola, a malcontent courtier, is hired by the brothers to discover the secret husband's identity, but the Duchess bears three children without anyone discovering who the father is. At the brothers' instigation, and under Bosola's supervision, the Duchess is imprisoned, subjected to mental persecution and eventually murdered, together with her maidservant Cariola and two of her children. Bosola, who has turned against the brothers after the Duchess's murder, accidentally kills Antonio. Bosola then stabs the Cardinal and kills Ferdinand (who has gone mad as a result of the Duchess's murder), but in the scuffle Ferdinand fatally wounds both Bosola and the Cardinal. The eldest child of Antonio and the Duchess survives, and Delio, Antonio's friend, plans to help him to gain his maternal inheritance.

The Renaissance Context

English Renaissance dramatists often used Italian court settings for their tragedies. Italy was the home of the Pope and the Catholic church and therefore an object of horrified fascination to a Protestant nation. It was also associated with the demonised figure of Machiavelli and with grotesque political and domestic intrigues, and it provided both an exotic location and a sufficiently coded medium for criticising the machinations of the English court without running a substantial risk of censorship. Also, stories based on real life Italian prototypes were readily available in collections like William Painter's *Palace of Pleasure* (1565-7), Webster's source, which was widely used by Renaissance dramatists looking for a good plot.

Webster is a more than competent verse dramatist, with a rich line in extended imagery of death, disease, deception and disguise, but he is also a master of the spare use of unornamented language. Many of the most famous lines in the play are stark in the way they encapsulate experience in simple phrases with very few adjectives or adverbs: 'I am Duchess of Malfi still'; 'Look you, the stars shine still'; 'When I look into the fish-ponds, in my garden,/Methinks I see a thing, arm'd with a rake/That seems to strike at me'. One critic has described Ferdinand's line 'Cover her face: mine eyes dazzle: she died young' as a three-act tragedy in miniature. As these examples suggest, Webster's dramatic method is emblematic, not only in the modern sense of deriving its effectiveness from visual as well as literary effects, but also in drawing on the Renaissance 'Emblem' tradition, where a woodcut

A Drama Classic

This edition of *The Duchess of Malfi* first published in Great Britain as a paperback original in 1996 by Nick Hern Books Limited, 14 Larden Road, London W3 7ST

Copyright in the introduction © 1996 Nick Hern Books Limited

The play text is reproduced from the 'Revels Plays' edition of *The Duchess of Malfi,* published by Manchester University Press, copyright © John Russell Brown 1974, by permission. The complete scholarly edition is available from Manchester University Press, Oxford Road, Manchester M13 9NR, UK

Typeset by Country Setting, Woodchurch, Kent TN26 3TB
Printed by BPC, Hazell Books Limited, Aylesbury HP20 1LB

A CIP catalogue record for this book is available from the British Library

ISBN 1 85459 215 7

Series editor: Kenneth McLeish

Associate editors:
Professor Trevor R. Griffiths, *School of Literary and Media Studies, University of North London*
Simon Trussler, *Reader in Drama, Goldsmiths' College, University of London*

cartoon would be coupled with a moral comment. Webster operates within a moralising tradition, as demonstrated by his use of beast fables like the Tale of the Salmon and the Dogfish at the end of 3.5 and his frequent use of *sententiae* (pithy moral statements, often in couplet form and often printed in italics, as in this edition), thus inviting responses to the play to resolve themselves into questions about how we are meant to regard the Duchess.

Although the general atmosphere of dark deeds done in shadow might suggest that the indoor Blackfriars theatre with its artificial lighting was an ideal venue, the King's Men also staged *The Duchess of Malfi* at the outdoor Globe as well. Technically the play is relatively straightforward: tableaux of dead bodies, a disembodied hand, a spectacular investiture and dances of madmen require no complicated apparatus. Richard Burbage (the original Hamlet) played Ferdinand, John Lowin was Bosola, Henry Condell the Cardinal. In keeping with the conventions of the period, the Duchess, Cariola, and Julia were played by young male actors; Richard Sharpe was the first Duchess. The original title page suggests that the play as printed was too long to be performed whole in the Renaissance: the published text included 'divers things printed that the length of the play would not bear in the presentment'. These may include the investiture of the Cardinal as a soldier, the banishment of the Duchess from Ancona, and perhaps Bosola's excoriation of the old woman, a set piece that contributes little to plot development in a naturalistic way, but does much to sum up a view of the world which is a key element in the play's exploration of deceit, treachery, and outward appearances.

The Duchess of Malfi: Melodrama or Tragedy?

The Duchess of Malfi can be extremely powerful in performance, but it has traditionally divided audiences and critics. Readers of the text may well find the play implausible, contrived and incoherent, whereas audiences at a production may find it a compellingly coherent presentation of an appallingly incoherent world. Is the play, as George Bernard Shaw argued, the work of a 'Tussaud laureate' indulging in horror for its own sake, or is it, as T. S. Eliot thought, the work of man who 'was much possessed by death/And saw the skull beneath the skin' and knew that 'thought clings round dead limbs/Tightening its lusts and luxuries'? The case against the play is that it is a series of melodramatic incidents violating both convention and probability, contrived to elicit incidental reactions of horror or pathos, wrapped up in creakily manufactured verse and limping to a macabre ending. The relationship between plausibility and sensation is problematic: is it credible that the Duchess bears three children without anyone working out who the father might be? Why does Webster let the Duchess think that her children are dead in one scene and then give her deathbed lines about their colds in another? The answer from those who see the play as a piece of melodramatic hokum has been that it gives Webster two opportunities to milk the children's deaths: first for horror and then for pathos. This approach is often tied up with a condemnation of the apparently bleakly nihilistic tendencies that pervade the play, which sit uneasily with some of the influential ideas about tragedy and realism fostered at the end of the nineteenth century by writers like Shaw. Those who wish to believe in an ordered, benevolent universe may find disturbing the play's refusal to offer solace beyond the bleakness of 'I am Duchess of Malfi still', and may seek to discredit this bleakness by denigrating Webster's skill as a playwright. Eliot's view, in contrast, is more in tune with a specifically twentieth century nihilism that can be seen to stem both from the almost casually monumental death rate amongst combatants in the First World War and from the revelations of civilian genocide in the Second World War, reinforced by the 'ethnic cleansing' of more recent conflicts. Webster's sequence of self-defining choices, his concentration on a search for some stable identity in the inner resources of the individual in *The Duchess of Malfi*, fits well with the outlook of such writers as Beckett, Sartre, and Camus with their ideas about the absurdity of human existence.

Plot and Character

Today, when playwrights often approach plot and character in ways derived from the naturalistic tradition in television, cinema, and (to a lesser extent) theatre, there is a powerful tendency to expect plays to be better organised than life, neatly revealing a manageable story presented through psychologically credible characters working towards a tidy resolution of conflict. These ideas actually reflect only a limited (and historically specific) view of what constitutes character, plot, or psychological credibility. Clearly, *The Duchess of Malfi* does not belong to the comparatively modern tradition of psychological realism. Webster's approach is closer to Brecht's than to Shaw's or Ibsen's: rather than moving smoothly from one well prepared climax to another, he proceeds by leaps from one key moment that crystallises a complex range of issues and debates to another. Perhaps his background in coachbuilding and his knowledge of Lord Mayor's Shows led him to a special awareness of the possibilities of dramatising scenes on a royal progress, though in this play it is an inverted progress, to destruction rather than triumph. *The Duchess of Malfi* is a play of set pieces, from the opening scene of Antonio describing the court, through to Delio asserting the claim of the surviving son in the final scene. These set pieces show the audience moments on the journey, but they do not necessarily show how the characters get there.

Sometimes the play is described as a 'revenge tragedy', a genre of which *Hamlet* is probably the best known example. But this ignores the classic revenge pattern where the revenger, like Hamlet, is aware from very early on who or what needs to be avenged and who the target is. In *The Duchess of Malfi* malevolent energies circulate relentlessly, seeking a person to attach themselves to. The way that Ferdinand responds to the Duchess hints that he has repressed feelings of incestuous sexuality towards her, and the revelation that they were twins suggests that he may be trying to achieve a sense of personal uniqueness by removing the obstacle she presents to his sense of individuality. Webster, however, does not present an unambiguous explanation for Ferdinand's pathological opposition to the Duchess. Similarly, while the Cardinal is presented in a way characteristic of Renaissance Protestant portraits of Catholic clergy, as a Machiavellian schemer, with a mistress and a neat line in espionage and murder, there is no clear sense of his motivation. Whereas Ferdinand goes spectacularly mad, dying with a moralising couplet on his lips, the Cardinal simply asks to be 'laid by, and never thought of', but their individual motivations can only be glimpsed, as Bosola puts it in another context, 'in a mist'.

In fact, the Duchess and Bosola are the only characters who can be seen as achieving the kind of self-knowledge that is associated with traditional notions of tragic catharsis. Even then, Bosola does not develop, in the manner of a naturalistic character, to some kind of redemptive self-awareness. A conflation of a number of different individuals in the source material, he is an amalgam of attitudes and positions who plays out a range of possible identities across the surface of the play, often appearing in physical as well as mental disguise: court malcontent (a traditional theatrical role), spy, and revenger. Plausibly interpreted by Bob Hoskins in Adrian Noble's excellent 1980 Manchester Royal Exchange production as a jocular, apparently streetwise operator who find himself out of his depth in a sea of conflicting emotions, Bosola is a channel for all the circulating passions of the play.

The Duchess

Unlike some Renaissance plays, *The Duchess* never vanished entirely from the stage: it was successful in the Restoration period, with Mr and Mrs Betterton as Bosola and the Duchess, and was adapted with some success on several occasions in the eighteenth and nineteenth centuries. William Poel's 1892 staging paved the way for a more sustained theatrical interest in the play that gathered momentum after the Second World War. The Duchess is now generally regarded as one of the great parts for a woman in Renaissance drama, and it has been memorably performed by Peggy Ashcroft, Helen Mirren, Juliet Stevenson, and Anastasia Hille among others. In performance, the Duchess is clearly a heroine: she provides us with a normative point of view that contrasts sharply with the diseased imaginations and bizarre behaviour that surrounds her. As is usually the case with Renaissance tragedy, she moves in a corrupt environment, dominated by her brothers, who exert a patriarchal power that turns the world to madness, death, and destruction. However, modern critics who read the play as endorsing this state of affairs have misread its theatrical dynamics. Certainly some thinkers of Webster's time did deplore widows' second marriages as examples of female lust, and some versions of the story do not take the Duchess's side. However, modern audiences confirm the testimony of Webster's dramatist colleagues in their commendatory verses to the play when they identify the Duchess as the object of their sympathy. Thomas Middleton, for example, wrote 'For who e'er saw this Duchess live, and die,/That could get off under a bleeding eye?' (i.e., without weeping).

The Duchess does attempt to operate as though she is living in what we might think of as a normal world, and she does clearly ignore her brother's prohibitions, but in performance her transgression offers the one positive model in a nightmare landscape. In a family whose other members are a Cardinal with a mistress who murders her with a poisoned bible, and an incestuous Duke who has the Duchess mentally tortured and murdered before going mad himself, the Duchess's domestic virtues shine out. Her death demonstrates the terrible fate of those who do transgress patriarchal lore and law, but to see the play as commending that patriarchal world view is to misunderstand the way that drama works. Within the play there is an example of precisely the lustful woman the brothers apparently think their sister is, in the shape of Julia, the Cardinal's mistress, but her behaviour contrasts sharply with the Duchess's.

The Duchess, as the play's tragic protagonist, tests the limits of the permissible on behalf of the audience. The horror of the play lies precisely in the narrowness of what her brothers will permit the Duchess to do and the disproportionate consequences that ensue. Even domesticity cannot survive the endemic violence of the play world, and the Duchess is tested to destruction. But her death shows the inadequacy of the world she has lived in, not of her modest claims to self-definition through marriage.

Trevor R. Griffiths, 1996

Key Dates

Pre-1580?	Born
1597	John Webster (probably the dramatist) enters the Middle Temple to study law
1602	Contributes to multi-authored plays: *Caesar's Fall* and *Christmas Comes But Once a Year* (now both lost), and *Lady Jane* (also known as *Sir Thomas Wyatt*)

1604	Writes Induction for (and probably additions to) Marston's *The Malcontent*
1605	Co-writes *Westward Ho* and *Northward Ho* with Dekker. Marries Sara Pennial?
1606	John Webster, son of the dramatist, baptised
1612	*The White Devil* acted; Webster contributes to Heywood's *An Apology for Actors*
1613?	*The Duchess of Malfi* acted
1615	Edits (and contributes to) third edition of Sir Thomas Overbury's *Characters*
1617	*The Devil's Law Case* acted
1622?	*Appius and Virginia* acted
Pre-1623	*The Guise* (now lost)
1624	Co-wrote *Keep the Widow Waking* (now lost); wrote Lord Mayor's Pageant *Monuments of Honour*; co-wrote *A Cure for a Cuckold*
Pre-1634	Dies

Further Reading

Because there is so little known about Webster, there is no full-scale biography, although M. C. Bradbrook's *John Webster: Citizen and Dramatist* (1980) rehearses the known facts and plausible inferences, provides a wealth of contextual information, and discusses the plays. G. K. and S. K. Hunter's *Penguin Critical Anthology, John Webster* (1969) is a mine of useful comment covering the period to 1964. *The Cambridge Companion to English Renaissance Drama* (eds. A. R. Braunmuller and Michael Hattaway, 1990) provides authoritative accounts of the social and theatrical contexts and guides to further reading. Kathleen McLuskie's *Renaissance Dramatists* (1989), an excellent general study of the period from a feminist perspective, has useful insights on the play, as does Alexander Leggatt's *English Drama: Shakespeare to the Restoration* (1988). Robert Browning's poem 'My Last Duchess' (1842) deals memorably with a similar theme.

THE DUCHESS OF MALFI

Dramatis Personae

FERDINAND, *Duke of Calabria, twin brother to the Duchess.*
THE CARDINAL, *their brother.*
DANIEL DE BOSOLA, *returned from imprisonment in the galleys following service for the Cardinal; later the Provisor of Horse to the Duchess, and in the pay of Ferdinand.*
ANTONIO BOLOGNA, *Steward of the Household to the Duchess; later her husband.*
DELIO, *his friend, a courtier.*
CASTRUCHIO, *an old lord; husband of Julia.*
MARQUIS OF PESCARA, *a soldier.*
COUNT MALATESTE, *a courtier at Rome.*
SILVIO, *a courtier at Malfi and Rome.*
RODERIGO,
GRISOLAN, *courtiers at Malfi.*
DOCTOR.

THE DUCHESS OF MALFI, *a young widow, later wife of Antonio, sister to the Cardinal and twin sister to Ferdinand.*
CARIOLA, *her waiting-woman.*
JULIA, *wife of Castruchio and mistress of the Cardinal.*
OLD LADY, *a midwife.*

Two Pilgrims.
Eight Madmen, *being an Astrologer, Lawyer, Priest, Doctor, English Tailor, Gentleman Usher, Farmer, and Broker.*
Court Officers; Servants; Guards; Executioners; Attendants; Churchmen.
Ladies-in-Waiting.

Scene: Malfi, Rome, Loretto, the countryside near Ancona, and Milan.

Act One, Scene One

Enter ANTONIO *and* DELIO.

DELIO. You are welcome to your country, dear Antonio –
    You have been long in France, and you return
    A very formal Frenchman in your habit.
    How do you like the French court?

ANTONIO.   I admire it –
    In seeking to reduce both state and people   5
    To a fix'd order, their judicious king
    Begins at home: quits first his royal palace
    Of flatt'ring sycophants, of dissolute
    And infamous persons – which he sweetly terms
    His Master's masterpiece, the work of heaven –   10
    Consid'ring duly, that a prince's court
    Is like a common fountain, whence should flow
    Pure silver drops in general: but if 't chance
    Some curs'd example poison 't near the head,
    Death, and diseases through the whole land spread.   15
    And what is 't makes this blessed government,
    But a most provident Council, who dare freely
    Inform him the corruption of the times?
    Though some o' th' court hold it presumption
    To instruct princes what they ought to do,   20
    It is a noble duty to inform them
    What they ought to foresee: –

Enter BOSOLA.

                   Here comes Bosola,
    The only court-gall: – yet I observe his railing
    Is not for simple love of piety;
    Indeed he rails at those things which he wants,   25

Would be as lecherous, covetous, or proud,
Bloody, or envious, as any man,
If he had means to be so: –

Enter CARDINAL.

                       Here's the cardinal.

BOSOLA. I do haunt you still.

CARDINAL.   So.

BOSOLA.   I have done you
   Better service than to be slighted thus: –   30
   Miserable age, where only the reward
   Of doing well, is the doing of it.

CARDINAL. You enforce your merit too much.

BOSOLA. I fell into the galleys in your service, where for two
   years together, I wore two towels instead of a shirt, with   35
   a knot on the shoulder, after the fashion of a Roman
   mantle: – slighted thus? I will thrive some way: black-
   birds fatten best in hard weather; why not I, in these
   dog-days?

CARDINAL. Would you could become honest.   40

BOSOLA. With all your divinity, do but direct me the way to
   it – [*Exit* CARDINAL.] I have known many travel far for it,
   and yet return as arrant knaves as they went forth, because
   they carried themselves always along with them; – Are you
   gone? Some fellows, they say, are possessed with the devil,   45
   but this great fellow were able to possess the greatest devil,
   and make him worse.

ANTONIO. He hath denied thee some suit?

BOSOLA. He, and his brother, are like plum-trees, that grow
   crooked over standing pools; they are rich, and o'erladen   50
   with fruit, but none but crows, pies, and caterpillars feed on
   them: could I be one of their flattering panders, I would hang
   on their ears like a horse-leech till I were full, and then drop
   off: – I pray leave me.

Who would rely upon these miserable dependences, in   55
expectation to be advanced tomorrow? what creature ever
fed worse than hoping Tantalus? nor ever died any man
more fearfully than he that hoped for a pardon. There are
rewards for hawks, and dogs, when they have done us service;
but for a soldier, that hazards his limbs in a battle, nothing   60
but a kind of geometry is his last supportation.

DELIO. Geometry?

BOSOLA. Ay, to hang in a fair pair of slings, take his latter swing
in the world upon an honourable pair of crutches, from hospital to hospital – fare ye well sir. And yet do not you scorn   65
us, for places in the court are but like beds in the hospital,
where this man's head lies at that man's foot, and so lower,
and lower.

[*Exit.*]

DELIO. I knew this fellow seven years in the galleys   70
For a notorious murder, and 'twas thought
The cardinal suborn'd it: he was releas'd
By the French general, Gaston de Foix,
When he recover'd Naples.

ANTONIO.   'Tis great pity
He should be thus neglected – I have heard   75
He's very valiant: this foul melancholy
Will poison all his goodness, for – I'll tell you –
If too immoderate sleep be truly said
To be an inward rust unto the soul,
It then doth follow want of action   80
Breeds all black malcontents, and their close rearing,
Like moths in cloth, do hurt for want of wearing.

Enter SILVIO, CASTRUCHIO, JULIA, RODERIGO,
and GRISOLAN.

DELIO. The presence 'gins to fill – you promis'd me
To make me the partaker of the natures
Of some of your great courtiers.

ANTONIO.   The Lord Cardinal's   85
   And other strangers', that are now in court?
   I shall: –

Enter FERDINAND.

                    Here comes the great Calabrian duke.

FERDINAND. Who took the ring oftenest?

SILVIO. Antonio Bologna, my lord.   89

FERDINAND. Our sister duchess' great master of her household?
   Give him the jewel: – When shall we leave this sportive action,
   and fall to action indeed?

CASTRUCHIO. Methinks, my lord, you should not desire to go to
   war in person.

FERDINAND. Now for some gravity! – why, my lord?   95

CASTRUCHIO. It is fitting a soldier arise to be a prince, but not
   necessary a prince descend to be a captain.

FERDINAND. No?

CASTRUCHIO. No, my lord, he were far better do it by a deputy.

FERDINAND. Why should he not as well sleep, or eat, by a   100
   deputy? This might take idle, offensive, and base office from
   him, whereas the other deprives him of honour.

CASTRUCHIO. Believe my experience: that realm is never long in
   quiet, where the ruler is a soldier.   104

FERDINAND. Thou told'st me thy wife could not endure fighting.

CASTRUCHIO. True, my lord.

FERDINAND. And of a jest she broke, of a captain she met full of
   wounds: – I have forgot it.

CASTRUCHIO. She told him, my lord, he was a pitiful fellow, to
   lie, like the children of Ishmael, all in tents.   110

FERDINAND. Why, there's a wit were able to undo all the
   chirurgeons o' the city, for although gallants should quarrel,

and had drawn their weapons, and were ready to go to it,
    yet her persuasions would make them put up.

CASTRUCHIO. That she would, my lord –   115

FERDINAND. How do you like my Spanish jennet?

RODERIGO. He is all fire.

FERDINAND. I am of Pliny's opinion, I think he was begot by the
    wind; he runs as if he were ballasted with quicksilver.

SILVIO. True, my lord, he reels from the tilt often.   120

RODERIGO, GRISOLAN. Ha, ha, ha!

FERDINAND. Why do you laugh? Methinks you that are
    courtiers should be my touch-wood, take fire, when I give
    fire; that is, laugh when I laugh, were the subject never so
    witty –   125

CASTRUCHIO. True, my lord, I myself have heard a very good
    jest, and have scorned to seem to have so silly a wit as to
    understand it.

FERDINAND. But I can laugh at your fool, my lord.

CASTRUCHIO. He cannot speak, you know, but he makes   130
    faces – my lady cannot abide him.

FERDINAND. No?

CASTRUCHIO. Nor endure to be in merry company: for she
    says too much laughing, and too much company, fills her
    too full of the wrinkle.   135

FERDINAND. I would then have a mathematical instrument
    made for her face, that she might not laugh out of compass: –
    I shall shortly visit you at Milan, Lord Silvio.

SILVIO. Your grace shall arrive most welcome.

FERDINAND. You are a good horseman, Antonio – you have   140
    excellent riders in France; what do you think of good
    horsemanship?

ANTONIO. Nobly, my lord – as out of the Grecian horse issued

many famous princes, so, out of brave horsemanship, arise
the first sparks of growing resolution, that raise the mind to   145
noble action.

FERDINAND. You have bespoke it worthily.

Enter CARDINAL, DUCHESS, CARIOLA, [*with*
ATTENDANTS].

SILVIO. Your brother, the Lord Cardinal, and sister Duchess.

CARDINAL. Are the galleys come about?

GRISOLAN. They are, my lord.   150

FERDINAND. Here's the Lord Silvio, is come to take his leave.

DELIO. Now sir, your promise: what's that cardinal?
I mean his temper? they say he's a brave fellow,
Will play his five thousand crowns at tennis, dance,
Court ladies, and one that hath fought single combats.   155

ANTONIO. Some such flashes superficially hang on him, for
form; but observe his inward character: – he is a melancholy
churchman; the spring in his face is nothing but the engen-
dering of toads; where he is jealous of any man, he lays worse
plots for them than ever was imposed on Hercules, for he   160
strews in his way flatterers, panders, intelligencers, atheists,
and a thousand such political monsters. He should have been
Pope; but instead of coming to it by the primitive decency of
the church, he did bestow bribes so largely, and so impudently,
as if he would have carried it away without heaven's know-   165
ledge. Some good he hath done.

DELIO. You have given too much of him: what's his brother?

ANTONIO. The duke there? a most perverse, and turbulent nature:
What appears in him mirth, is merely outside;   170
If he laugh heartily, it is to laugh
All honesty out of fashion.

DELIO.   Twins?

ANTONIO.   In quality: –

He speaks with others' tongues, and hears men's suits
With others' ears; will seem to sleep o' th' bench
Only to entrap offenders in their answers;   175
Dooms men to death by information,
Rewards by hearsay.

DELIO.   Then the law to him
  Is like a foul black cobweb to a spider –
  He makes it his dwelling, and a prison
  To entangle those shall feed him.

ANTONIO.   Most true: 180
  He ne'er pays debts, unless they be shrewd turns,
  And those he will confess that he doth owe.
  Last, for his brother, there, the cardinal –
  They that do flatter him most say oracles
  Hang at his lips: and verily I believe them;   185
  For the devil speaks in them.
  But for their sister, the right noble duchess –
  You never fix'd your eye on three fair medals,
  Cast in one figure, of so different temper:
  For her discourse, it is so full of rapture   190
  You only will begin then to be sorry
  When she doth end her speech; and wish, in wonder,
  She held it less vain-glory to talk much,
  Than you penance to hear her: whilst she speaks,
  She throws upon a man so sweet a look,   195
  That it were able raise one to a galliard
  That lay in a dead palsy, and to dote
  On that sweet countenance: but in that look,
  There speaketh so divine a continence
  As cuts off all lascivious, and vain hope.   200
  Her days are practis'd in such noble virtue
  That sure her nights – nay more, her very sleeps –
  Are more in heaven than other ladies' shrifts.
  Let all sweet ladies break their flatt'ring glasses,
  And dress themselves in her.

DELIO.   Fie Antonio,   205
  You play the wire-drawer with her commendations.

ANTONIO. I'll case the picture up: – only thus much –
    All her particular worth grows to this sum:
    She stains the time past, lights the time to come.

CARIOLA. You must attend my lady, in the gallery,   210
    Some half an hour hence.

ANTONIO. I shall.

FERDINAND. Sister, I have a suit to you: –

DUCHESS.   To me, sir?

FERDINAND. A gentleman here, Daniel de Bosola;
    One that was in the galleys.

DUCHESS.   Yes, I know him: –   215

FERDINAND. A worthy fellow h' is: pray let me entreat for
    The provisorship of your horse.

DUCHESS.   Your knowledge of him
    Commends him, and prefers him.

FERDINAND.   Call him hither –

    [*Exit* ATTENDANT.]

    We now are upon parting: good Lord Silvio,
    Do us commend to all our noble friends   220
    At the leaguer.

SILVIO.   Sir, I shall.

DUCHESS.   You are for Milan?

SILVIO. I am: –

DUCHESS. Bring the caroches: we'll bring you down to the haven.

    [*Exeunt all except* CARDINAL *and* FERDINAND.]

CARDINAL. Be sure you entertain that Bosola
    For your intelligence: I would not be seen in 't;   225
    And therefore many times I have slighted him
    When he did court our furtherance, as this morning.

FERDINAND. Antonio, the great master of her household
    Had been far fitter –

CARDINAL.   You are deceiv'd in him,

Enter BOSOLA.

    His nature is too honest for such business –   230
    He comes: I'll leave you. [*Exit.*]

BOSOLA.   I was lur'd to you.

FERDINAND. My brother here, the cardinal, could never
    Abide you.

BOSOLA.   Never since he was in my debt.

FERDINAND. May be some oblique character in your face
    Made him suspect you!

BOSOLA.   Doth he study physiognomy?   235
    There's no more credit to be given to th' face
    Than to a sick man's urine, which some call
    The physician's whore, because she cozens him: –
    He did suspect me wrongfully.

FERDINAND.   For that
    You must give great men leave to take their times: 240
    Distrust doth cause us seldom be deceiv'd; --
    You see, the oft shaking of the cedar-tree
    Fastens it more at root.

BOSOLA.   Yet take heed:
    For to suspect a friend unworthily
    Instructs him the next way to suspect you,   245
    And prompts him to deceive you.

FERDINAND.   There's gold.

BOSOLA.   So:
    What follows? Never rain'd such show'rs as these
    Without thunderbolts in the tail of them;
    Whose throat must I cut?

FERDINAND. Your inclination to shed blood rides post   250

Before my occasion to use you: – I give you that
To live i' th' court, here; and observe the duchess,
To note all the particulars of her 'haviour;
What suitors do solicit her for marriage
And whom she best affects: she's a young widow –   255
I would not have her marry again.

BOSOLA.   No, sir?

FERDINAND. Do not you ask the reason: but be satisfied,
I say I would not.

BOSOLA.   It seems you would create me
One of your familiars.

FERDINAND.   Familiar! what's that?

BOSOLA. Why, a very quaint invisible devil, in flesh: 260
An intelligencer.

FERDINAND.   Such a kind of thriving thing
I would wish thee: and ere long, thou mayst arrive
At a higher place by 't.

BOSOLA.   Take your devils
Which hell calls angels: these curs'd gifts would make
You a corrupter, me an impudent traitor,   265
And should I take these they'd take me to hell.

FERDINAND. Sir, I'll take nothing from you that I have given: –
There is a place that I procur'd for you
This morning: the provisorship o' th' horse –
Have you heard on 't?

BOSOLA.   No.

FERDINAND.   'Tis yours – is' t not worth thanks? 270

BOSOLA. I would have you curse yourself now, that your bounty,
Which makes men truly noble, e'er should make
Me a villain: O, that to avoid ingratitude
For the good deed you have done me, I must do
All the ill man can invent! Thus the devil   275
Candies all sins o'er; and what heaven terms vile,

That names he complimental.

FERDINAND.   Be yourself:
  Keep your old garb of melancholy; 'twill express
  You envy those that stand above your reach,
  Yet strive not to come near 'em: this will gain   280
  Access to private lodgings, where yourself
  May, like a politic dormouse –

BOSOLA.   As I have seen some
  Feed in a lord's dish, half asleep, not seeming
  To listen to any talk; and yet these rogues
  Have cut his throat in a dream: – what's my place?   285
  The provisorship o' th' horse? say then, my corruption
  Grew out of horse-dung: I am your creature.

FERDINAND. Away.

BOSOLA. Let good men, for good deeds, covet good fame,
  Since place and riches oft are bribes of shame –   290
  Sometimes the devil doth preach.

    Exit. [*Enter* DUCHESS *and* CARDINAL.]

CARDINAL. We are to part from you: and your own discretion
  Must now be your director.

FERDINAND.   You are a widow:
  You know already what man is; and therefore
  Let not youth, high promotion, eloquence –   295

CARDINAL. No, nor anything without the addition, honour,
  Sway your high blood.

FERDINAND.   Marry! they are most luxurious
  Will wed twice.

CARDINAL.   O fie!

FERDINAND.   Their livers are more spotted
  Than Laban's sheep.

DUCHESS.   Diamonds are of most value
  They say, that have pass'd through most jewellers' hands.   300

FERDINAND. Whores, by that rule, are precious: –

DUCHESS.   Will you hear me?
   I'll never marry: –

CARDINAL.   So most widows say:
   But commonly that motion lasts no longer
   Than the turning of an hour-glass – the funeral sermon
   And it, end both together.

FERDINAND.   Now hear me: 305
   You live in a rank pasture here, i' th' court –
   There is a kind of honey-dew that's deadly:
   'Twill poison your fame; look to 't: be not cunning:
   For they whose faces do belie their hearts
   Are witches, ere they arrive at twenty years –   310
   Ay: and give the devil suck.

DUCHESS. This is terrible good counsel: –

FERDINAND. Hypocrisy is woven of a fine small thread,
   Subtler than Vulcan's engine: yet, believe 't,
   Your darkest actions – nay, your privat'st thoughts –   315
   Will come to light.

CARDINAL.   You may flatter yourself,
   And take your own choice: privately be married
   Under the eaves of night.

FERDINAND.   Think 't the best voyage
   That e'er you made; like the irregular crab,
   Which though 't goes backward, thinks that it goes right,   320
   Because it goes its own way: but observe,
   Such weddings may more properly be said
   To be executed, than celebrated.

CARDINAL. The marriage night
   Is the entrance into some prison.

FERDINAND.   And those joys,   325
   Those lustful pleasures, are like heavy sleeps
   Which do fore-run man's mischief –

CARDINAL.   Fare you well.
    Wisdom begins at the end: remember it. [*Exit.*]

DUCHESS. I think this speech between you both was studied,
    It came so roundly off.

FERDINAND.   You are my sister –   330
    This was my father's poniard: do you see?
    I'd be loth to see 't look rusty, 'cause 'twas his: –
    I would have you to give o'er these chargeable revels;
    A visor and a mask are whispering-rooms
    That were ne'er built for goodness: fare ye well: –   335
    And women like that part which, like the lamprey,
    Hath ne'er a bone in 't.

DUCHESS.   Fie sir!

FERDINAND.   Nay,
    I mean the tongue: variety of courtship; –
    What cannot a neat knave with a smooth tale
    Make a woman believe? Farewell, lusty widow. [*Exit.*]   340

DUCHESS. Shall this move me? If all my royal kindred
    Lay in my way unto this marriage,
    I'd make them my low footsteps: and even now,
    Even in this hate, as men in some great battles,
    By apprehending danger, have achiev'd   345
    Almost impossible actions – I have heard soldiers say so –
    So I, through frights, and threat'nings, will assay
    This dangerous venture: let old wives report
    I wink'd and chose a husband. Cariola,

    [*Enter* CARIOLA.]

    To thy known secrecy I have given up   350
    More than my life, my fame: –

CARDINAL. Both shall be safe:
    For I'll conceal this secret from the world
    As warily as those that trade in poison
    Keep poison from their children.

DUCHESS.   Thy protestation

Is ingenious and hearty: I believe it.   355
Is Antonio come?

CARIOLA.   He attends you: –

DUCHESS.   Good dear soul,
Leave me: but place thyself behind the arras,
Where thou mayst overhear us: – wish me good speed
For I am going into a wilderness,
Where I shall find nor path, nor friendly clew   360
To be my guide.

　　[CARIOLA *withdraws behind the arras. Enter* ANTONIO.]

          I sent for you – sit down:
Take pen and ink, and write: are you ready?

ANTONIO.   Yes

DUCHESS. What did I say?

ANTONIO.   That I should write somewhat

DUCHESS. O, I remember: –
After these triumphs, and this large expense,   365
It's fit, like thrifty husbands, we inquire
What's laid up for tomorrow.

ANTONIO. So please your beauteous excellence.

DUCHESS.   Beauteous?
Indeed I thank you: I look young for your sake
You have ta'en my cares upon you.

ANTONIO.   I'll fetch your grace   370
The particulars of your revenue, and expense.

DUCHESS. O, you are an upright treasurer: but you mistook,
For when I said I meant to make inquiry
What's laid up for tomorrow, I did mean
What's laid up yonder for me.

ANTONIO.   Where?

DUCHESS.   In heaven –   375
I am making my will (as 'tis fit princes should,

In perfect memory), and I pray sir, tell me
Were not one better make it smiling, thus,
Than in deep groans, and terrible ghastly looks,
As if the gifts we parted with procur'd   380
That violent distraction?

ANTONIO.   O, much better.

DUCHESS. If I had a husband now, this care were quit:
　　But I intend to make you overseer; –
　　What good deed shall we first remember? say.

ANTONIO. Begin with that first good deed began i' th' world   385
　　After man's creation, the sacrament of marriage –
　　I'd have you first provide for a good husband,
　　Give him all.

DUCHESS.   All?

ANTONIO.   Yes, your excellent self.

DUCHESS. In a winding sheet?

ANTONIO.   In a couple.

DUCHESS. Saint Winifred, that were a strange will!   390

ANTONIO. 'Twere strange if there were no will in you
　　To marry again.

DUCHESS.   What do you think of marriage?

ANTONIO. I take 't, as those that deny purgatory –
　　It locally contains, or heaven, or hell;
　　There's no third place in 't.

DUCHESS.   How do you affect it?   395

ANTONIO. My banishment, feeding my melancholy,
　　Would often reason thus . . .

DUCHESS.   Pray let's hear it.

ANTONIO. Say a man never marry, nor have children,
　　What takes that from him? only the bare name
　　Of being a father, or the weak delight   400

> To see the little wanton ride a-cock-horse
> Upon a painted stick, or hear him chatter
> Like a taught starling.

DUCHESS.   Fie, fie, what's all this?
    One of your eyes is blood-shot – use my ring to 't,
    They say 'tis very sovereign – 'twas my wedding ring,   405
    And I did vow never to part with it,
    But to my second husband.

ANTONIO. You have parted with it now.

DUCHESS. Yes, to help your eyesight.

ANTONIO. You have made me stark blind.   410

DUCHESS. How?

ANTONIO. There is a saucy, and ambitious devil
    Is dancing in this circle.

DUCHESS.   Remove him.

ANTONIO.   How?

DUCHESS. There needs small conjuration, when your finger
    May do it: thus – is it fit?

    [*She puts her ring upon his finger:*] *he kneels.*

ANTONIO.   What said you?

DUCHESS.   Sir,   415
    This goodly roof of yours is too low built,
    I cannot stand upright in 't, nor discourse,
    Without I raise it higher: raise yourself,
    Or if you please, my hand to help you: so. [*Raises him.*]

ANTONIO. Ambition, madam, is a great man's madness,   420
    That is not kept in chains, and close-pent rooms,
    But in fair lightsome lodgings, and is girt
    With the wild noise of prattling visitants,
    Which makes it lunatic, beyond all cure –
    Conceive not I am so stupid but I aim   425
    Whereto your favours tend: but he's a fool

That, being a-cold, would thrust his hands i' th' fire
To warm them.

DUCHESS.   So, now the ground's broke,
    You may discover what a wealthy mine
    I make you lord of.

ANTONIO.   O, my unworthiness!   430

DUCHESS. You were ill to sell yourself –
    This dark'ning of your worth is not like that
    Which tradesmen use i' th' city; their false lights
    Are to rid bad wares off: and I must tell you
    If you will know where breathes a complete man –   435
    I speak it without flattery – turn your eyes
    And progress through yourself.

ANTONIO. Were there nor heaven nor hell,
    I should be honest: I have long serv'd virtue,
    And ne'er ta'en wages of her.

DUCHESS.   Now she pays it!   440
    The misery of us that are born great –
    We are forc'd to woo, because none dare woo us:
    And as a tyrant doubles with his words,
    And fearfully equivocates, so we
    Are forc'd to express our violent passions   445
    In riddles, and in dreams, and leave the path
    Of simple virtue, which was never made
    To seem the thing it is not. Go, go brag
    You have left me heartless – mine is in your bosom,
    I hope 'twill multiply love there. You do tremble: 450
    Make not your heart so dead a piece of flesh
    To fear, more than to love me: sir, be confident –
    What is 't distracts you? This is flesh, and blood, sir;
    'Tis not the figure cut in alabaster
    Kneels at my husband's tomb. Awake, awake, man!   455
    I do here put off all vain ceremony,
    And only do appear to you a young widow
    That claims you for her husband, and like a widow,
    I use but half a blush in 't.

ANTONIO.   Truth speak for me:
   I will remain the constant sanctuary   460
   Of your good name.

DUCHESS.   I thank you, gentle love,
   And 'cause you shall not come to me in debt,
   Being now my steward, here upon your lips
   I sign your *Quietus est:* – [*Kisses him.*]
   This you should have begg'd now –   465
   I have seen children oft eat sweetmeats thus,
   As fearful to devour them too soon.

ANTONIO. But for your brothers?

DUCHESS.   Do not think of them –
   All discord, without this circumference,
   Is only to be pitied, and not fear'd: 470
   Yet, should they know it, time will easily
   Scatter the tempest.

ANTONIO.   These words should be mine,
   And all the parts you have spoke, if some part of it
   Would not have savour'd flattery.

DUCHESS. Kneel.

   [CARIOLA *comes from behind the arras.*]   475

ANTONIO. Hah?

DUCHESS. Be not amaz'd, this woman's of my counsel –
   I have heard lawyers say, a contract in a chamber
   Per verba de presenti is absolute marriage: –
   Bless, heaven, this sacred Gordian, which let violence   480
   Never untwine.

ANTONIO. And may our sweet affections, like the spheres,
   Be still in motion.

DUCHESS.   Quickening, and make
   The like soft music.

ANTONIO. That we may imitate the loving palms,   485
   Best emblem of a peaceful marriage,

That ne'er bore fruit, divided.

DUCHESS. What can the church force more?

ANTONIO. That Fortune may not know an accident,
    Either of joy or sorrow, to divide   490
    Our fixed wishes.

DUCHESS.   How can the church bind faster?
    We now are man and wife, and 'tis the church
    That must but echo this: – maid, stand apart –
    I now am blind.

ANTONIO.   What's your conceit in this?

DUCHESS. I would have you lead your fortune by the hand,   495
    Unto your marriage bed: –
    (You speak in me this, for we now are one)
    We'll only lie, and talk together, and plot
    T'appease my humorous kindred; and if you please,
    Like the old tale, in 'Alexander and Lodowick',   500
    Lay a naked sword between us, keep us chaste: –
    O, let me shroud my blushes in your bosom,
    Since 'tis the treasury of all my secrets.

    [*Exeunt* DUCHESS *and* ANTONIO.]

CARIOLA. Whether the spirit of greatness or of woman
    Reign most in her, I know not, but it shows   505
    A fearful madness; I owe her much of pity.

    Exit.

Act Two, Scene One

Enter BOSOLA *and* CASTRUCHIO.

BOSOLA. You say you would fain be taken for an eminent courtier?

CASTRUCHIO. 'Tis the very main of my ambition.

BOSOLA. Let me see, you have a reasonable good face for 't
    already, and your night-cap expresses your ears sufficient
    largely – I would have you learn to twirl the strings of your   5
    band with a good grace; and in a set speech, at th' end of
    every sentence, to hum, three or four times, or blow your
    nose till it smart again, to recover your memory; when you
    come to be a president in criminal causes, if you smile
    upon a prisoner, hang him, but if you frown upon him and   10
    threaten him, let him be sure to 'scape the gallows.

CASTRUCHIO. I would be a very merry president –

BOSOLA. Do not sup o' nights, 'twill beget you an admirable wit.

CASTRUCHIO. Rather it would make me have a good stomach
    to quarrel, for they say your roaring boys eat meat seldom,   15
    and that makes them so valiant. But how shall I know whether
    the people take me for an eminent fellow?

BOSOLA. I will teach a trick to know it: give out you lie a-dying,
    and if you hear the common people curse you, be sure you are
    taken for one of the prime night-caps –   20

Enter an OLD LADY.

You come from painting now?

OLD LADY. From what?

BOSOLA. Why, from your scurvy face-physic – to behold thee
    not painted inclines somewhat near a miracle: these, in thy

face here, were deep ruts and foul sloughs the last progress.   25
There was a lady in France, that having had the smallpox,
flayed the skin off her face to make it more level; and whereas
before she looked like a nutmeg-grater, after she resembled an
abortive hedgehog.

OLD LADY. Do you call this painting?   30

BOSOLA. No, no, but careening of an old morphewed lady, to
     make her disembogue again – there's rough-cast phrase to your
     plastic.

OLD LADY. It seems you are well acquainted with my closet.

BOSOLA. One would suspect it for a shop of witchcraft, to find   35
     in it the fat of serpents, spawn of snakes, Jews' spittle, and their
     young children's ordure – and all these for the face: I would
     sooner eat a dead pigeon, taken from the soles of the feet of
     one sick of the plague, than kiss one of you fasting. Here are
     two of you, whose sin of your youth is the very patrimony of   40
     the physician, makes him renew his footcloth with the spring
     and change his high-prized courtezan with the fall of the leaf:
     I do wonder you do not loathe yourselves – observe my
     meditation now:

What thing is in this outward form of man   45
To be belov'd? we account it ominous
If nature do produce a colt, or lamb,
A fawn, or goat, in any limb resembling
A man; and fly from 't as a prodigy.
Man stands amaz'd to see his deformity   50
In any other creature but himself.
But in our own flesh, though we bear diseases
Which have their true names only ta'en from beasts,
As the most ulcerous wolf, and swinish measle;
Though we are eaten up of lice and worms,   55
And though continually we bear about us
A rotten and dead body, we delight
To hide it in rich tissue: all our fear –
Nay, all our terror – is lest our physician
Should put us in the ground, to be made sweet.   60

Your wife's gone to Rome: you two couple, and get you to the
wells at Lucca, to recover your aches.

[*Exeunt* CASTRUCHIO *and* OLD LADY.]

I have other work on foot: – I observe our duchess
Is sick o' days, she pukes, her stomach seethes,
The fins of her eyelids look most teeming blue,   65
She wanes i' th' cheek, and waxes fat i' th' flank;
And (contrary to our Italian fashion)
Wears a loose-body'd gown – there's somewhat in 't!
I have a trick may chance discover it,
A pretty one: I have bought some apricocks,   70
The first our spring yields.

Enter ANTONIO *and* DELIO [*, talking apart*].

DELIO.   And so long since married?
    You amaze me.

ANTONIO.   Let me seal your lips for ever,
    For did I think that anything but th' air
    Could carry these words from you, I should wish
    You had no breath at all: –   75

    [*To* BOSOLA.] Now sir, in your contemplation? You are
    studying to become a great wise fellow?

BOSOLA. O sir, the opinion of wisdom is a foul tetter that runs
    all over a man's body: if simplicity direct us to have no evil, it
    directs us to a happy being; for the subtlest folly proceeds   80
    from the subtlest wisdom: let me be simply honest.

ANTONIO. I do understand your inside.

BOSOLA. Do you so?

ANTONIO. Because you would not seem to appear to the world
    puffed up with your preferment, you continue this out-of-   85
    fashion melancholy – leave it, leave it.

BOSOLA. Give me leave to be honest in any phrase, in any
    compliment whatsoever – shall I confess myself to you?
    I look no higher than I can reach: they are the gods that

must ride on winged horses; a lawyer's mule of a slow pace   90
will both suit my disposition and business: for mark me, when
a man's mind rides faster than his horse can gallop, they
quickly both tire.

ANTONIO. You would look up to heaven, but I think
    The devil, that rules i' th' air, stands in your light.   95

BOSOLA. O sir, you are lord of the ascendant, chief man with the
    duchess, a duke was your cousin-german removed: – say you
    were lineally descended from King Pepin, or he himself, what
    of this? search the heads of the greatest rivers in the world,
    you shall find them but bubbles of water. Some would think   100
    the souls of princes were brought forth by some more weighty
    cause than those of meaner persons – they are deceived, there's
    the same hand to them: the like passions sway them, the same
    reason that makes a vicar go to law for a tithe-pig and undo his
    neighbours, makes them spoil a whole province, and batter   105
    down goodly cities with the cannon.

    Enter DUCHESS [*with* ATTENDANTS *and* LADIES].

DUCHESS. Your arm Antonio – do I not grow fat?
    I am exceeding short-winded: – Bosola,
    I would have you, sir, provide for me a litter,   110
    Such a one as the Duchess of Florence rode in.

BOSOLA. The duchess us'd one when she was great with child.

DUCHESS. I think she did: – Come hither, mend my ruff –
    Here, when? thou art such a tedious lady; and
    Thy breath smells of lemon pills – would thou hadst done –   115
    Shall I swoon under thy fingers? I am
    So troubled with the mother.

BOSOLA [*aside*].   I fear too much.

DUCHESS. I have heard you say that the French courtiers
    Wear their hats on 'fore the king.

ANTONIO.   I have seen it.

DUCHESS. In the presence?   120

ANTONIO. Yes: –

DUCHESS.   Why should not we bring up that fashion?
  'Tis ceremony more than duty, that consists
  In the removing of a piece of felt:
  Be you the example to the rest o' th' court,
  Put on your hat first.

ANTONIO.   You must pardon me: 125
  I have seen, in colder countries than in France,
  Nobles stand bare to th' prince; and the distinction
  Methought show'd reverently.

BOSOLA. I have a present for your grace.

DUCHESS.   For me sir?

BOSOLA. Apricocks, madam.

DUCHESS.   O sir, where are they?   130
  I have heard of none to-year.

BOSOLA [aside].   Good, her colour rises.

DUCHESS. Indeed I thank you; they are wondrous fair ones:
  What an unskilful fellow is our gardener!
  We shall have none this month.

BOSOLA. Will not your grace pare them?   135

DUCHESS. No, they taste of musk, methinks; indeed they do: –

BOSOLA. I know not: yet I wish your grace had par'd 'em: –

DUCHESS. Why?

BOSOLA.   I forgot to tell you the knave gard'ner
  (Only to raise his profit by them the sooner)
  Did ripen them in horse-dung.

DUCHESS.   O you jest: –   140
  You shall judge; pray taste one.

ANTONIO.   Indeed madam
  I do not love the fruit.

DUCHESS.   Sir, you are loth

To rob us of our dainties: – 'tis a delicate fruit,
They say they are restorative.

BOSOLA.   'Tis a pretty art,
  This grafting.

DUCHESS.   'Tis so: a bettering of nature.   145

BOSOLA. To make a pippin grow upon a crab,
  A damson on a blackthorn: – [*Aside.*] how greedily she eats them!
  A whirlwind strike off these bawd farthingales,
  For, but for that, and the loose-body'd gown,
  I should have discover'd apparently   150
  The young springal cutting a caper in her belly.

DUCHESS. I thank you, Bosola, they were right good ones –
  If they do not make me sick.

ANTONIO.   How now madam?

DUCHESS. This green fruit and my stomach are not friends –
  How they swell me!

BOSOLA [*aside*].   Nay, you are too much swell'd already.   155

DUCHESS. O, I am in an extreme cold sweat!

BOSOLA. I am very sorry: –

DUCHESS. Lights to my chamber: O good Antonio,
  I fear I am undone.

  Exit.

DELIO.   Lights there, lights!

  [*Exeunt all except* ANTONIO *and* DELIO.]

ANTONIO. O my most trusty Delio, we are lost!   160
  I fear she's fall'n in labour; and there's left
  No time for her remove.

DELIO.   Have you prepar'd
  Those ladies to attend her? and procur'd
  That politic safe conveyance for the midwife
  Your duchess plotted?   165

ANTONIO. I have: –

DELIO.   Make use then of this forc'd occasion:
  Give out that Bosola hath poison'd her
  With these apricocks; that will give some colour
  For her keeping close.

ANTONIO.   Fie, fie, the physicians
  Will then flock to her.

DELIO.   For that you may pretend   170
  She'll use some prepar'd antidote of her own,
  Lest the physicians should re-poison her.

ANTONIO. I am lost in amazement: I know not what to think on 't.

  Exeunt.

Act Two, Scene Two

Enter BOSOLA.

BOSOLA. So, so: there's no question but her tetchiness and
  most vulturous eating of the apricocks are apparent signs of
  breeding –

  Enter OLD LADY.

  Now?

OLD LADY. I am in haste, sir.   5

BOSOLA. There was a young waiting-woman had a monstrous
  desire to see the glass-house.

OLD LADY. Nay, pray let me go: –

BOSOLA. And it was only to know what strange instrument it
  was should swell up a glass to the fashion of a woman's belly. 10

OLD LADY. I will hear no more of the glass-house – you are still
  abusing women!

BOSOLA. Who I? no, only (by the way now and then) mention
  your frailties. The orange tree bears ripe and green fruit, and
  blossoms all together: and some of you give entertainment   15
  for pure love; but more, for more precious reward. The lusty
  spring smells well; but drooping autumn tastes well: if we have
  the same golden showers that rained in the time of Jupiter
  the Thunderer, you have the same Danaës still, to hold up
  their laps to receive them: – didst thou never study the   20
  mathematics?

OLD LADY. What's that, sir?

BOSOLA. Why, to know the trick how to make a many lines
  meet in one centre: – go, go; give your foster-daughters good
  counsel: tell them that the devil takes delight to hang at a   25
  woman's girdle, like a false rusty watch, that she cannot
  discern how the time passes.

  [*Exit* OLD LADY.]

  Enter ANTONIO, DELIO, RODERIGO, GRISOLAN.

ANTONIO. Shut up the court gates: –

RODERIGO.   Why sir? what's the danger?

ANTONIO. Shut up the posterns presently: and call
  All the officers o' th' court.

GRISOLAN.   I shall instantly. [*Exit*.]   30

ANTONIO. Who keeps the key o' th' park gate?

RODERIGO.   Forobosco.

ANTONIO. Let him bring 't presently.

  Enter [GRISOLAN *with*] OFFICERS.

FIRST OFFICER. O, gentlemen o' th' court, the foulest treason!

BOSOLA [*aside*]. If that these apricocks should be poison'd now,
  Without my knowledge!   35

FIRST OFFICER. There was taken even now a Switzer in the
  duchess' bedchamber.

SECOND OFFICER. A Switzer?

FIRST OFFICER. With a pistol in his great cod-piece.

BOSOLA. Ha, ha, ha!   40

FIRST OFFICER. The cod-piece was the case for 't.

SECOND OFFICER. There was a cunning traitor. Who would
   have searched his cod-piece?

FIRST OFFICER. True, if he had kept out of the ladies' chambers:
   – and all the moulds of his buttons were leaden bullets.   45

SECOND OFFICER. O, wicked cannibal! a fire-lock in's cod-piece!

FIRST OFFICER. 'Twas a French plot, upon my life.

SECOND OFFICER. To see what the devil can do!

ANTONIO. All the officers here?

OFFICERS. We are: –   50

ANTONIO. Gentlemen,
   We have lost much plate you know; and but this evening
   Jewels, to the value of four thousand ducats
   Are missing in the duchess' cabinet –
   Are the gates shut?

OFFICERS.   Yes.

ANTONIO.   'Tis the duchess' pleasure   55
   Each officer be lock'd into his chamber
   Till the sun-rising; and to send the keys
   Of all their chests, and of their outward doors,
   Into her bedchamber: – she is very sick.

RODERIGO. At her pleasure.   60

ANTONIO. She entreats you take 't not ill: the innocent
   Shall be the more approv'd by it.

BOSOLA. Gentleman o' th' wood-yard, where's your Switzer now?

FIRST OFFICER. By this hand, 'twas credibly reported by one
   o' the black guard.   65

[*Exeunt all except* ANTONIO *and* DELIO.]

DELIO. How fares it with the duchess?

ANTONIO.   She's expos'd
　　Unto the worst of torture, pain, and fear: –

DELIO. Speak to her all happy comfort.

ANTONIO. How I do play the fool with mine own danger!
　　You are this night, dear friend, to post to Rome;   70
　　My life lies in your service.

DELIO.   Do not doubt me –

ANTONIO. O, 'tis far from me: and yet fear presents me
　　Somewhat that looks like danger.

DELIO.   Believe it,
　　'Tis but the shadow of your fear, no more:
　　How superstitiously we mind our evils!   75
　　The throwing down salt, or crossing of a hare,
　　Bleeding at nose, the stumbling of a horse,
　　Or singing of a cricket, are of pow'r
　　To daunt whole man in us. Sir, fare you well:
　　I wish you all the joys of a bless'd father;   80
　　And, for my faith, lay this unto your breast –
　　Old friends, like old swords, still are trusted best. [*Exit.*]

　　Enter CARIOLA.

CARIOLA. Sir, you are the happy father of a son –
　　Your wife commends him to you.

ANTONIO.   Blessed comfort:
　　For heaven-sake tend her well; I'll presently   85
　　Go set a figure for's nativity.

　　Exeunt.

Act Two, Scene Three

Enter BOSOLA[, *with a dark lantern*].

BOSOLA. Sure I did hear a woman shriek: list, hah?
　　And the sound came, if I receiv'd it right,
　　From the duchess' lodgings: there's some stratagem
　　In the confining all our courtiers
　　To their several wards: I must have part of it,　　　　5
　　My intelligence will freeze else: – list again!
　　It may be 'twas the melancholy bird,
　　Best friend of silence and of solitariness,
　　The owl, that scream'd so: –

Enter ANTONIO.

　　　　　　　　　　　　　　hah? Antonio!　　　　　9

ANTONIO. I heard some noise: who's there? what art thou? speak.

BOSOLA. Antonio? Put not your face nor body
　　To such a forc'd expression of fear –
　　I am Bosola; your friend.

ANTONIO.　　　　　　　　Bosola! –
　　[*Aside.*] This mole does undermine me – [*To him.*] heard you not
　　A noise even now?

BOSOLA.　　　　　　From whence?

ANTONIO.　　　　　　　　　　　From the duchess' lodging.　15

BOSOLA. Not I: did you?

ANTONIO.　　　　　　I did: or else I dream'd.

BOSOLA. Let's walk towards it.

ANTONIO.　　　　　　　　No: it may be 'twas
　　But the rising of the wind: –

BOSOLA.　　　　　　　　Very likely.
　　Methinks 'tis very cold, and yet you sweat:
　　You look wildly.

ANTONIO.　　　　I have been setting a figure　　　20
　　For the duchess' jewels: –

BOSOLA.   Ah: and how falls your question?
  Do you find it radical?

ANTONIO.   What's that to you?
  'Tis rather to be question'd what design,
  When all men were commanded to their lodgings,
  Makes you a night-walker.

BOSOLA.   In sooth I'll tell you: 25
  Now all the court's asleep, I thought the devil
  Had least to do here; I came to say my prayers –
  And if it do offend you I do so,
  You are a fine courtier.

ANTONIO [aside].   This fellow will undo me: –
  [To him.] You gave the duchess apricocks today,   30
  Pray heaven they were not poison'd!

BOSOLA.   Poison'd! a Spanish fig
  For the imputation.

ANTONIO.   Traitors are ever confident,
  Till they are discover'd: – there were jewels stol'n too –
  In my conceit, none are to be suspected
  More than yourself.

BOSOLA.   You are a false steward.   35

ANTONIO. Saucy slave! I'll pull thee up by the roots; –

BOSOLA. May be the ruin will crush you to pieces.

ANTONIO. You are an impudent snake indeed, sir,
  Are you scarce warm, and do you show your sting?

  [BOSOLA's line is missing in the original: presumably an insult.]

ANTONIO. You libel well, sir.

BOSOLA.   No sir, copy it out,   40
  And I will set my hand to 't.

ANTONIO [aside].   My nose bleeds
  One that were superstitious would count
  This ominous; – when it merely comes by chance.

Two letters, that are wrought here for my name,
Are drown'd in blood!   45
Mere accident: – [*To him.*] for you, sir, I'll take order:
I' th' morn you shall be safe: – [*Aside.*] 'tis that must colour
Her lying-in: – [*To him.*] sir, this door you pass not:
I do not hold it fit that you come near
The duchess' lodgings, till you have quit yourself.   50
[*Aside.*] *The great are like the base – nay, they are the same –*
When they seek shameful ways, to avoid shame.

Exit.

BOSOLA. Antonio hereabout did drop a paper –
Some of your help, false friend – O, here it is:
What's here? a child's nativity calculated!   55

[*Reads.*] *The duchess was delivered of a son, 'tween the*
hours twelve and one, in the night: Anno Dom. 1504, –
that's this year – *decimo nono Decembris,* – that's this
night – *taken according to the meridian of Malfi* – that's
our duchess: happy discovery! – *The lord of the first*   60
house, being combust in the ascendant, signifies short life: and
Mars being in a human sign, joined to the tail of the Dragon,
in the eighth house, doth threaten a violent death, caetera non
scrutantur.

Why now 'tis most apparent: this precise fellow   65
Is the duchess' bawd: – I have it to my wish;
This is a parcel of intelligency
Our courtiers were cas'd up for! It needs must follow
That I must be committed on pretence
Of poisoning her; which I'll endure, and laugh at: –   70
If one could find the father now! but that
Time will discover. Old Castruchio
I' th' morning posts to Rome; by him I'll send
A letter, that shall make her brothers' galls
O'erflow their livers – this was a thrifty way.   75
Though lust do mask in ne'er so strange disguise,
She's oft found witty, but is never wise. [*Exit.*]

Act Two, Scene Four

Enter CARDINAL *and* JULIA.

CARDINAL. Sit: thou art my best of wishes – prithee tell me
    What trick didst thou invent to come to Rome
    Without thy husband.

JULIA.   Why, my lord, I told him
    I came to visit an old anchorite
    Here, for devotion.

CARDINAL.   Thou art a witty false one: –   5
    I mean to him.

JULIA.   You have prevail'd with me
    Beyond my strongest thoughts: I would not now
    Find you inconstant.

CARDINAL.   Do not put thyself
    To such a voluntary torture, which proceeds
    Out of your own guilt.

JULIA.   How, my lord?

CARDINAL.   You fear   10
    My constancy, because you have approv'd
    Those giddy and wild turnings in yourself.

JULIA. Did you e'er find them?

CARDINAL.   Sooth, generally for women:
    A man might strive to make glass malleable,
    Ere he should make them fixed.

JULIA.   So, my lord –   15

CARDINAL. We had need go borrow that fantastic glass
    Invented by Galileo the Florentine,
    To view another spacious world i' th' moon
    And look to find a constant woman there.

JULIA. This is very well, my lord.

CARDINAL.   Why do you weep?   20
    Are tears your justification? the self-same tears

Will fall into your husband's bosom, lady,
With a loud protestation, that you love him
Above the world: – come, I'll love you wisely,
That's jealously, since I am very certain   25
You cannot me make cuckold.

JULIA.   I'll go home
    To my husband.

CARDINAL.   You may thank me, lady,
    I have taken you off your melancholy perch,
    Bore you upon my fist, and show'd you game,
    And let you fly at it: – I pray thee kiss me –   30
    When thou wast with thy husband, thou wast watch'd
    Like a tame elephant: – still you are to thank me –
    Thou hadst only kisses from him, and high feeding,
    But what delight was that? 'twas just like one
    That hath a little fing'ring on the lute,   35
    Yet cannot tune it: – still you are to thank me.

JULIA. You told me of a piteous wound i' th' heart,
    And a sick liver, when you woo'd me first,
    And spake like one in physic.

CARDINAL.   Who's that? –
    Rest firm: for my affection to thee,   40
    Lightning moves slow to 't.

    Enter SERVANT.

SERVANT.   Madam, a gentleman,
    That's come post from Malfi, desires to see you.

CARDINAL. Let him enter, I'll withdraw.

    Exit.

SERVANT.   He says,
    Your husband, old Castruchio, is come to Rome,
    Most pitifully tir'd with riding post. [*Exit.*]   45

    Enter DELIO.

JULIA [*aside*]. Signior Delio! 'tis one of my old suitors.

DELIO. I was bold to come and see you.

JULIA.   Sir, you are welcome.

DELIO. Do you lie here?

JULIA.   Sure, your own experience
    Will satisfy you, no – our Roman prelates
    Do not keep lodging for ladies.

DELIO.   Very well: 50
    I have brought you no commendations from your husband,
    For I know none by him.

JULIA.   I hear he's come to Rome?

DELIO. I never knew man and beast, of a horse and a knight,
    So weary of each other – if he had had a good back,
    He would have undertook to have borne his horse,   55
    His breech was so pitifully sore.

JULIA.   Your laughter
    Is my pity.

DELIO.   Lady, I know not whether
    You want money, but I have brought you some.

JULIA. From my husband?

DELIO.   No, from mine own allowance.

JULIA. I must hear the condition, ere I be bound to take it.   60

DELIO. Look on 't, 'tis gold – hath it not a fine colour?

JULIA. I have a bird more beautiful.

DELIO. Try the sound on 't.

JULIA.   A lute-string far exceeds it;
    It hath no smell, like cassia or civet,
    Nor is it physical, though some fond doctors   65
    Persuade us seethe 't in cullises – I'll tell you,
    This is a creature bred by . . .

[*Enter* SERVANT.]

SERVANT.   Your husband's come,
   Hath deliver'd a letter to the Duke of Calabria,
   That, to my thinking, hath put him out of his wits. [*Exit.*]

JULIA. Sir, you hear –   70
   Pray let me know your business and your suit,
   As briefly as can be.

DELIO.   With good speed – I would wish you
   (At such time as you are non-resident
   With your husband) my mistress.

JULIA. Sir, I'll go ask my husband if I shall,   75
   And straight return your answer.

   Exit.

DELIO.   Very fine!
   Is this her wit or honesty that speaks thus?
   I heard one say the duke was highly mov'd
   With a letter sent from Malfi: – I do fear
   Antonio is betray'd. How fearfully   80
   Shows his ambition now! unfortunate fortune!
   They pass through whirlpools and deep woes do shun,
   Who the event weigh, ere the action's done.

   Exit.

Act Two, Scene Five

Enter CARDINAL, *and* FERDINAND *with a letter.*

FERDINAND. I have this night digg'd up a mandrake.

CARDINAL.   Say you?

FERDINAND. And I am grown mad with 't.

CARDINAL.   What's the prodigy?

FERDINAND. Read there – a sister damn'd; she's loose i' th' hilts:
   Grown a notorious strumpet.

CARDINAL.   Speak lower.

FERDINAND.   Lower?   5
  Rogues do not whisper 't now, but seek to publish 't
  (As servants do the bounty of their lords)
  Aloud; and with a covetous searching eye
  To mark who note them: – O confusion seize her!
  She hath had most cunning bawds to serve her turn,
  And more secure conveyances for lust   10
  Than towns of garrison for service.

CARDINAL.   Is' t possible?
  Can this be certain?

FERDINAND.   Rhubarb, O for rhubarb
  To purge this choler! here's the cursed day
  To prompt my memory, and here 't shall stick
  Till of her bleeding heart I make a sponge   15
  To wipe it out.

CARDINAL. Why do you make yourself
  So wild a tempest?

FERDINAND.   Would I could be one,
  That I might toss her palace 'bout her ears,
  Root up her goodly forests, blast her meads,
  And lay her general territory as waste   20
  As she hath done her honours.

CARDINAL.   Shall our blood,
  The royal blood of Arragon and Castile,
  Be thus attainted?

FERDINAND.   Apply desperate physic:
  We must not now use balsamum, but fire,
  The smarting cupping-glass, for that's the mean   25
  To purge infected blood, such blood as hers: –
  There is a kind of pity in mine eye,
  I'll give it to my handkercher; and now 'tis here,
  I'll bequeath this to her bastard.

CARDINAL.   What to do?

FERDINAND. Why, to make soft lint for his mother's wounds,   30
  When I have hew'd her to pieces.

CARDINAL.   Curs'd creature!
  Unequal nature, to place women's hearts
  So far upon the left side!

FERDINAND.   Foolish men,
  That e'er will trust their honour in a bark
  Made of so slight, weak bulrush as is woman,   35
  Apt every minute to sink it!

CARDINAL. Thus ignorance, when it hath purchas'd honour,
  It cannot wield it.

FERDINAND.   Methinks I see her laughing –
  Excellent hyena! – talk to me somewhat, quickly,
  Or my imagination will carry me   40
  To see her, in the shameful act of sin.

CARDINAL. With whom?

FERDINAND.   Happily with some strong thigh'd bargeman;
  Or one o' th' wood-yard, that can quoit the sledge,
  Or toss the bar, or else some lovely squire
  That carries coals up to her privy lodgings.   45

CARDINAL. You fly beyond your reason.

FERDINAND.   Go to, mistress!
  'Tis not your whore's milk that shall quench my wild-fire,
  But your whore's blood.

CARDINAL. How idly shows this rage! which carries you,
  As men convey'd by witches through the air,   50
  On violent whirlwinds – this intemperate noise
  Fitly resembles deaf men's shrill discourse,
  Who talk aloud, thinking all other men
  To have their imperfection.

FERDINAND.   Have not you
  My palsy?

CARDINAL. Yes – I can be angry   55

Without this rupture: there is not in nature
A thing that makes man so deform'd, so beastly,
As doth intemperate anger: – chide yourself.
You have divers men who never yet express'd
Their strong desire of rest, but by unrest,   60
By vexing of themselves: – come, put yourself
In tune.

FERDINAND. So; I will only study to seem
The thing I am not. I could kill her now,
In you, or in myself, for I do think
It is some sin in us, heaven doth revenge   65
By her.

CARDINAL. Are you stark mad?

FERDINAND.   I would have their bodies
Burnt in a coal-pit, with the ventage stopp'd,
That their curs'd smoke might not ascend to heaven:
Or dip the sheets they lie in, in pitch or sulphur,
Wrap them in 't, and then light them like a match;   70
Or else to boil their bastard to a cullis,
And give 't his lecherous father, to renew
The sin of his back.

CARDINAL.   I'll leave you.

FERDINAND.   Nay, I have done –
I am confident, had I been damn'd in hell
And should have heard of this, it would have put me   75
Into a cold sweat: – In, in; I'll go sleep –
Till I know who leaps my sister, I'll not stir:
That known, I'll find scorpions to string my whips,
And fix her in a general eclipse.

   Exeunt.

Act Three, Scene One

Enter ANTONIO *and* DELIO.

ANTONIO. Our noble friend, my most beloved Delio!
    O, you have been a stranger long at court –
    Came you along with the Lord Ferdinand?

DELIO. I did sir; and how fares your noble duchess?

ANTONIO. Right fortunately well: she's an excellent   5
    Feeder of pedigrees; since you last saw her,
    She hath had two children more, a son and daughter.

DELIO. Methinks 'twas yesterday: let me but wink,
    And not behold your face, which to mine eye
    Is somewhat leaner, verily I should dream   10
    It were within this half-hour.

ANTONIO. You have not been in law, friend Delio,
    Nor in prison, nor a suitor at the court,
    Nor begg'd the reversion of some great man's place,
    Nor troubled with an old wife, which doth make   15
    Your time so insensibly hasten.

DELIO.   Pray sir, tell me,
    Hath not this news arriv'd yet to the ear
    Of the Lord Cardinal?

ANTONIO.   I fear it hath –
    The Lord Ferdinand, that's newly come to court,
    Doth bear himself right dangerously.

DELIO.   Pray why?   20

ANTONIO. He is so quiet, that he seems to sleep
    The tempest out, as dormice do in winter:
    Those houses that are haunted are most still,

Till the devil be up.

DELIO.   What say the common people?

ANTONIO. The common rabble do directly say   25
  She is a strumpet.

DELIO.   And your graver heads,
  Which would be politic, what censure they?

ANTONIO. They do observe I grow to infinite purchase
  The left-hand way, and all suppose the duchess
  Would amend it, if she could: for, say they,   30
  Great princes, though they grudge their officers
  Should have such large and unconfined means
  To get wealth under them, will not complain
  Lest thereby they should make them odious
  Unto the people – for other obligation   35
  Of love, or marriage, between her and me,
  They never dream of.

  Enter FERDINAND *and* DUCHESS.

DELIO.   The Lord Ferdinand
  Is going to bed.

FERDINAND.   I'll instantly to bed,
  For I am weary: – I am to bespeak
  A husband for you.

DUCHESS.   For me, sir! pray who is' t?   40

FERDINAND. The great Count Malateste.

DUCHESS.   Fie upon him, –
  A count! he's a mere stick of sugar-candy,
  You may look quite thorough him: when I choose
  A husband, I will marry for your honour.   44

FERDINAND. You shall do well in 't: – how is' t, worthy Antonio?

DUCHESS. But sir, I am to have private conference with you
  About a scandalous report, is spread
  Touching mine honour.

FERDINAND.   Let me be ever deaf to 't:
  One of Pasquil's paper bullets, court-calumny,
  A pestilent air which princes' palaces   50
  Are seldom purg'd of: yet, say that it were true, –
  I pour it in your bosom – my fix'd love
  Would strongly excuse, extenuate, nay, deny
  Faults, were they apparent in you: go be safe
  In your own innocency.

DUCHESS.   O bless'd comfort!   55
  This deadly air is purg'd.

  Exeunt [all except FERDINAND].

FERDINAND.   Her guilt treads on
  Hot-burning coulters: –

  Enter BOSOLA.

                Now Bosola,
  How thrives our intelligence?

BOSOLA.   Sir, uncertainly:
  'Tis rumour'd she hath had three bastards, but
  By whom, we may go read i' th' stars.

FERDINAND.   Why some   60
  Hold opinion, all things are written there.

BOSOLA. Yes, if we could find spectacles to read them –
  I do suspect there hath been some sorcery
  Us'd on the duchess.

FERDINAND.   Sorcery! to what purpose?

BOSOLA. To make her dote on some desertless fellow   65
  She shames to acknowledge.

FERDINAND.   Can your faith give way
  To think there's pow'r in potions, or in charms,
  To make us love, whether we will or no?

BOSOLA. Most certainly.

FERDINAND. Away, these are mere gulleries, horrid things   70
    Invented by some cheating mountebanks
    To abuse us: – do you think that herbs or charms
    Can force the will? Some trials have been made
    In this foolish practice; but the ingredients
    Were lenitive poisons, such as are of force   75
    To make the patient mad; and straight the witch
    Swears, by equivocation, they are in love.
    The witchcraft lies in her rank blood: this night
    I will force confession from her. You told me
    You had got, within these two days, a false key   80
    Into her bed-chamber.

BOSOLA.   I have.

FERDINAND.   As I would wish.

BOSOLA. What do you intend to do?

FERDINAND.   Can you guess?

BOSOLA.   No: –

FERDINAND. Do not ask then:
    He that can compass me, and know my drifts,
    May say he hath put a girdle 'bout the world   85
    And sounded all her quicksands.

BOSOLA.   I do not
    Think so.

FERDINAND. What do you think then? pray?

BOSOLA.   That you
    Are your own chronicle too much; and grossly
    Flatter yourself.

FERDINAND.   Give me thy hand, I thank thee:
    I never gave pension but to flatterers,   90
    Till I entertained thee. Farewell:
    That friend a great man's ruin strongly checks
    Who rails into his belief all his defects.

    Exeunt.

Act Three. Scene Two

Enter DUCHESS, ANTONIO *and* CARIOLA.

DUCHESS. Bring me the casket hither, and the glass: –
    You get no lodging here tonight, my lord.

ANTONIO. Indeed, I must persuade one: –

DUCHESS.   Very good:
    I hope in time 'twill grow into a custom
    That noblemen shall come with cap and knee,   5
    To purchase a night's lodging of their wives.

ANTONIO. I must lie here.

DUCHESS.   Must? you are a lord of mis-rule.

ANTONIO. Indeed, my rule is only in the night.

DUCHESS. To what use will you put me?

ANTONIO.   We'll sleep together: –

DUCHESS. Alas, what pleasure can two lovers find in sleep?   10

CARIOLA. My lord, I lie with her often; and I know
    She'll much disquiet you: –

ANTONIO.   See, you are complain'd of.

CARIOLA. For she's the sprawling'st bedfellow.

ANTONIO. I shall like her the better for that.

CARIOLA. Sir, shall I ask you a question   15

ANTONIO. I pray thee, Cariola.

CARIOLA. Wherefore still when you lie with my lady
    Do you rise so early?

ANTONIO.   Labouring men
    Count the clock oft'nest Cariola,
    Are glad when their task's ended.

DUCHESS.   I'll stop your mouth.   20

    [*Kisses him.*]

ANTONIO. Nay, that's but one – Venus had two soft doves
    To draw her chariot: I must have another.

[*Kisses her.*]

    When wilt thou marry, Cariola?

CARIOLA.   Never, my lord.

ANTONIO. O fie upon this single life! forgo it!
    We read how Daphne, for her peevish fight,   25
    Became a fruitless bay-tree; Syrinx turn'd
    To the pale empty reed; Anaxarete
    Was frozen into marble: whereas those
    Which marry'd, or prov'd kind unto their friends,
    Were, by a gracious influence, transshap'd   30
    Into the olive, pomegranate, mulberry;
    Became flow'rs, precious stones, or eminent stars.

CARIOLA. This is a vain poetry: but I pray you tell me,
    If there were propos'd me, wisdom, riches, and beauty,
    In three several young men, which should I choose?   35

ANTONIO. 'Tis a hard question: this was Paris' case
    And he was blind in 't, and there was great cause;
    For how was 't possible he could judge right,
    Having three amorous goddesses in view,
    And they stark naked? 'twas a motion   40
    Were able to benight the apprehension
    Of the severest counsellor of Europe.
    Now I look on both your faces so well form'd,
    It puts me in mind of a question I would ask.

CARIOLA. What is' t?

ANTONIO.   I do wonder why hard-favour'd ladies,   45
    For the most part, keep worse-favour'd waiting-women
    To attend them, and cannot endure fair ones.

DUCHESS. O, that's soon answer'd.
    Did you ever in your life know an ill painter
    Desire to have his dwelling next door to the shop   50
    Of an excellent picture-maker? 'twould disgrace

His face-making, and undo him: – I prithee,
When were we so merry? – my hair tangles.

ANTONIO. Pray thee, Cariola, let's steal forth the room
 And let her talk to herself; I have divers times   55
 Serv'd her the like, when she hath chaf'd extremely:
 I love to see her angry: – softly, Cariola.

 Exit with CARIOLA.

DUCHESS. Doth not the colour of my hair 'gin to change?
 When I wax gray, I shall have all the court
 Powder their hair with arras, to be like me: –   60
 You have cause to love me; I enter'd you into my heart
 Before you would vouchsafe to call for the keys.

 Enter FERDINAND [*behind*].

 We shall one day have my brothers take you napping:
 Methinks his presence, being now in court,
 Should make you keep your own bed; but you'll say 65
 Love mix'd with fear is sweetest. I'll assure you
 You shall get no more children till my brothers
 Consent to be your gossips: – have you lost your tongue?

 [*Turns and sees* FERDINAND.]

 'Tis welcome: For know, whether I am doom'd to live or die, 70
 I can do both like a prince.

 FERDINAND *gives her a poniard.*

FERDINAND.   Die then, quickly!
 Virtue, where art thou hid? what hideous thing
 Is it that doth eclipse thee?

DUCHESS.   Pray sir, hear me: –

FERDINAND. Or is it true, thou art but a bare name,
 And no essential thing?

DUCHESS.   Sir: –

FERDINAND.   Do not speak.

DUCHESS.   No sir: 75

I will plant my soul in mine ears to hear you.

FERDINAND. O most imperfect light of human reason,
    That mak'st us so unhappy, to foresee
    What we can least prevent! Pursue thy wishes,
    And glory in them: there's in shame no comfort   80
    But to be past all bounds, and sense of shame.

DUCHESS. I pray sir, hear me: I am married.

FERDINAND.   So: –

DUCHESS. Happily, not to your liking: but for that,
    Alas, your shears do come untimely now
    To clip the bird's wings that's already flown!   85
    Will you see my husband?

FERDINAND.   Yes, if I could change
    Eyes with a basilisk: –

DUCHESS.   Sure, you came hither
    By his confederacy.

FERDINAND.   The howling of a wolf
    Is music to thee, screech-owl, prithee peace!
    Whate'er thou art, that hast enjoy'd my sister, –   90
    For I am sure thou hear'st me – for thine own sake
    Let me not know thee: I came hither prepar'd
    To work thy discovery, yet am now persuaded
    It would beget such violent effects
    As would damn us both: – I would not for ten millions   95
    I had beheld thee; therefore use all means
    I never may have knowledge of thy name;
    Enjoy thy lust still, and a wretched life,
    On that condition. – And for thee, vile woman,
    If thou do wish thy lecher may grow old   100
    In thy embracements, I would have thee build
    Such a room for him as our anchorites
    To holier use inhabit: let not the sun
    Shine on him, till he's dead; let dogs and monkeys
    Only converse with him, and such dumb things   105
    To whom nature denies use to sound his name;

Do not keep a paraquito, lest she learn it.
If thou do love him, cut out thine own tongue
Lest it bewray him.

DUCHESS.   Why might not I marry?
I have not gone about, in this, to create   110
Any new world, or custom.

FERDINAND.   Thou art undone:
And thou hast ta'en that massy sheet of lead
That hid thy husband's bones, and folded it
About my heart.

DUCHESS.   Mine bleeds for 't.

FERDINAND.   Thine? thy heart?
What should I name 't, unless a hollow bullet   115
Fill'd with unquenchable wild-fire?

DUCHESS.   You are, in this,
Too strict: and were you not my princely brother
I would say too wilful: my reputation
Is safe.

FERDINAND. Dost thou know what reputation is?
I'll tell thee – to small purpose, since th' instruction   120
Comes now too late:
Upon a time, Reputation, Love, and Death
Would travel o'er the world; and it was concluded
That they should part, and take three several ways:
Death told them, they should find him in great battles,   125
Or cities plagu'd with plagues; Love gives them counsel
To inquire for him 'mongst unambitious shepherds,
Where dowries were not talk'd of, and sometimes
'Mongst quiet kindred that had nothing left
By their dead parents: 'Stay', quoth Reputation,   130
'Do not forsake me; for it is my nature
If once I part from any man I meet
I am never found again.' And so, for you:
You have shook hands with Reputation,
And made him invisible: – so fare you well.   135
I will never see you more.

DUCHESS. Why should only I,
    Of all the other princes of the world,
    Be cas'd up, like a holy relic? I have youth,
    And a little beauty.

FERDINAND.   So you have some virgins   140
    That are witches: – I will never see thee more.

Exit.

Enter ANTONIO *with a pistol*[*, and* CARIOLA].

DUCHESS. You saw this apparition?

ANTONIO.   Yes: we are
    Betray'd; how came he hither? I should turn
    This to thee, for that.

CARIOLA.   Pray sir, do: and when
    That you have cleft my heart, you shall read there   145
    Mine innocence.

DUCHESS.   That gallery gave him entrance.

ANTONIO. I would this terrible thing would come again,
    That, standing on my guard, I might relate
    My warrantable love: –

She shews the poniard.

                ha, what means this?

DUCHESS. He left this with me: –

ANTONIO.   And it seems did wish   150
    You would use it on yourself?

DUCHESS.   His action seem'd
    To intend so much.

ANTONIO.   This hath a handle to 't
    As well as a point – turn it towards him,
    And so fasten the keen edge in his rank gall: –

[*Knocking within.*]

How now! who knocks? more earthquakes?

DUCHESS.   I stand   155
  As if a mine, beneath my feet, were ready
  To be blown up.

CARIOLA.   'Tis Bosola: –

DUCHESS.   Away!
  O misery! methinks unjust actions
  Should wear these masks and curtains, and not we: –
  You must instantly part hence; I have fashion'd it already.   160

Exit ANTONIO.

Enter BOSOLA.

BOSOLA. The duke your brother is ta'en up in a whirlwind,
  Hath took horse, and's rid post to Rome.

DUCHESS.   So late?

BOSOLA. He told me, as he mounted into th' saddle,
  You were undone.

DUCHESS.   Indeed, I am very near it.

BOSOLA. What's the matter?   165

DUCHESS. Antonio, the master of our household,
  Hath dealt so falsely with me, in's accounts:
  My brother stood engag'd with me for money
  Ta'en up of certain Neapolitan Jews,
  And Antonio lets the bonds be forfeit.   170

BOSOLA. Strange! – [*Aside.*] This is cunning: –

DUCHESS.   And hereupon
  My brother's bills at Naples are protested
  Against: – call up our officers.

BOSOLA.   I shall.

  Exit.

  [*Enter* ANTONIO.]

DUCHESS. The place that you must fly to is Ancona,
  Hire a house there. I'll send after you   175

My treasure and my jewels: our weak safety
Runs upon enginous wheels; short syllables
Must stand for periods. I must now accuse you
Of such a feigned crime as Tasso calls
Magnanima menzogna: a noble lie   180
'Cause it must shield our honours: – hark! they are coming.

Enter [BOSOLA *and*] OFFICERS.

ANTONIO. Will your grace hear me?

DUCHESS. I have got well by you: you have yielded me
    A million of loss; I am like to inherit
    The people's curses for your stewardship.   185
    You had the trick in audit-time to be sick,
    Till I had sign'd your *quietus;* and that cur'd you
    Without help of a doctor. – Gentlemen,
    I would have this man be an example to you all:
    So shall you hold my favour; I pray let him,   190
    For h' as done that, alas, you would not think of,
    And, because I intend to be rid of him,
    I mean not to publish: – use your fortune elsewhere.

ANTONIO. I am strongly arm'd to brook my overthrow,
    As commonly men bear with a hard year: 195
    I will not blame the cause on 't; but do think
    The necessity of my malevolent star
    Procures this, not her humour. O the inconstant
    And rotten ground of service! – you may see:
    'Tis ev'n like him, that in a winter night   200
    Takes a long slumber o'er a dying fire,
    As loth to part from 't; yet parts thence as cold
    As when he first sat down.

DUCHESS.   We do confiscate,
    Towards the satisfying of your accounts,
    All that you have.   205

ANTONIO. I am all yours: and 'tis very fit
    All mine should be so.

DUCHESS.   So, sir; you have your pass.

ANTONIO. You may see, gentlemen, what 'tis to serve
  A prince with body, and soul.

  Exit.

BOSOLA. Here's an example, for extortion: what moisture is   210
  drawn out of the sea, when foul weather comes, pours down
  and runs into the sea again.

DUCHESS. I would know what are your opinions of this Antonio.

SECOND OFFICER. He could not abide to see a pig's head
  gaping: I thought your grace would find him a Jew.   215

THIRD OFFICER. I would you had been his officer, for your own
  sake.

FOURTH OFFICER. You would have had more money.

FIRST OFFICER. He stopp'd his ears with black wool; and to
  those came to him for money, said he was thick of hearing.   220

SECOND OFFICER. Some said he was an hermaphrodite, for he
  could not abide a woman.

FOURTH OFFICER. How scurvy proud he would look, when
  the treasury was full! Well, let him go: –

FIRST OFFICER. Yes, and the chippings of the buttery fly after
  him, to scour his gold chain.   225

DUCHESS. Leave us.

  Exeunt OFFICERS.

  What do you think of these?

BOSOLA. That these are rogues, that in's prosperity,
  But to have waited on his fortune, could have wish'd
  His dirty stirrup riveted through their noses,   230
  And follow'd after's mule, like a bear in a ring;
  Would have prostituted their daughters to his lust;
  Made their first-born intelligencers; thought none happy
  But such as were born under his bless'd planet,
  And wore his livery: and do these lice drop off now?   235
  Well, never look to have the like again:

He hath left a sort of flatt'ring rogues behind him –

He hath left a sort of flatt'ring rogues behind him –
Their doom must follow: princes pay flatterers
In their own money; flatterers dissemble their vices
And they dissemble their lies: that's justice –   240
Alas, poor gentleman!

DUCHESS. Poor? he hath amply fill'd his coffers.

BOSOLA.   Sure
He was too honest: Pluto, the god of riches,
When he's sent by Jupiter to any man
He goes limping, to signify that wealth   245
That comes on god's name comes slowly: but when he's sent
On the devil's errand, he rides post and comes in by scuttles.
Let me show you what a most unvalu'd jewel
You have, in a wanton humour, thrown away,
To bless the man shall find him: he was an excellent   250
Courtier, and most faithful, a soldier that thought it
As beastly to know his own value too little
As devilish to acknowledge it too much:
Both his virtue and form deserv'd a far better fortune.
His discourse rather delighted to judge itself, than show itself. 255
His breast was fill'd with all perfection,
And yet it seem'd a private whisp'ring-room,
It made so little noise of 't.

DUCHESS.   But he was basely descended.

BOSOLA. Will you make yourself a mercenary herald,
Rather to examine men's pedigrees than virtues?   260
You shall want him,
For know an honest statesman to a prince
Is like a cedar, planted by a spring:
The spring bathes the tree's root, the grateful tree
Rewards it with his shadow: you have not done so –   265
I would sooner swim to the Bermudas on
Two politicians' rotten bladders, tied
Together with an intelligencer's heart-string,
Than depend on so changeable a prince's favour.
Fare thee well, Antonio; since the malice of the world   270

Would needs down with thee, it cannot be said yet
That any ill happened unto thee,
Considering thy fall was accompanied with virtue.

DUCHESS. O, you render me excellent music.

BOSOLA.   Say you?

DUCHESS. This good one that you speak of, is my husband.   275

BOSOLA. Do I not dream? can this ambitious age
Have so much goodness in 't, as to prefer
A man merely for worth, without these shadows
Of wealth, and painted honours? possible?

DUCHESS. I have had three children by him.

BOSOLA.   Fortunate lady!   280
For you have made your private nuptial bed
The humble and fair seminary of peace:
No question but many an unbenefic'd scholar
Shall pray for you for this deed, and rejoice
That some preferment in the world can yet   285
Arise from merit. The virgins of your land
That have no dowries, shall hope your example
Will raise them to rich husbands: should you want
Soldiers, 'twould make the very Turks and Moors
Turn Christians, and serve you for this act.   290
Last, the neglected poets of your time,
In honour of this trophy of a man,
Rais'd by that curious engine, your white hand,
Shall thank you, in your grave, for 't; and make that
More reverend than all the cabinets   295
Of living princes. For Antonio,
His fame shall likewise flow from many a pen,
When heralds shall want coats to sell to men.

DUCHESS. As I taste comfort in this friendly speech,
So would I find concealment.   300

BOSOLA. O, the secret of my prince,
Which I will wear on th' inside of my heart.

DUCHESS. You shall take charge of all my coin and jewels,

And follow him; for he retires himself
  To Ancona.

BOSOLA.   So.

DUCHESS.   Whither, within few days,   305
  I mean to follow thee.

BOSOLA.   Let me think:
  I would wish your grace to feign a pilgrimage
  To our Lady of Loretto, scarce seven leagues
  From fair Ancona; so may you depart
  Your country with more honour, and your flight   310
  Will seem a princely progress, retaining
  Your usual train about you.

DUCHESS.   Sir, your direction
  Shall lead me by the hand.

CARIOLA.   In my opinion,
  She were better progress to the baths
  At Lucca, or go visit the Spa   315
  In Germany, for, if you will believe me,
  I do not like this jesting with religion,
  This feigned pilgrimage.

DUCHESS. Thou art a superstitious fool –
  Prepare us instantly for our departure: 320
  Past sorrows, let us moderately lament them,
  For those to come, seek wisely to prevent them.

  Exit [with CARIOLA].

BOSOLA. A politician is the devil's quilted anvil –
  He fashions all sins on him, and the blows
  Are never heard: he may work in a lady's chamber,   325
  As here for proof what rests, but I reveal
  All to my lord? O, this base quality
  Of intelligencer! why, every quality i' th' world
  Prefers but gain or commendation:
  Now, for this act I am certain to be rais'd,   330
  And men that paint weeds to the life are prais'd.

  Exit.

Act Three, Scene Three

Enter CARDINAL *with* MALATESTE, FERDINAND *with* DELIO
and SILVIO, *and* PESCARA.

CARDINAL. Must we turn soldier then?

MALATESTE.   The Emperor,
    Hearing your worth that way, ere you attain'd
    This reverend garment, joins you in commission
    With the right fortunate soldier, the Marquis of Pescara,
    And the famous Lannoy.

CARDINAL. He that had the honour   5
    Of taking the French king prisoner?

MALATESTE.   The same –
    Here's a plot drawn for a new fortification
    At Naples.

FERDINAND. This great Count Malateste, I perceive,
    Hath got employment?

DELIO.   No employment, my lord;   10
    A marginal note in the muster-book, that he is
    A voluntary lord.

FERDINAND.   He's no soldier?

DELIO. He has worn gunpowder in's hollow tooth,
    For the toothache.

SILVIO. He comes to the leaguer with a full intent   15
    To eat fresh beef and garlic, means to stay
    Till the scent be gone, and straight return to court.

DELIO. He hath read all the late service
    As the City Chronicle relates it,
    And keeps two painters going, only to express   20
    Battles in model.

SILVIO.   Then he'll fight by the book.

DELIO. By the almanac, I think –
    To choose good days, and shun the critical.

That's his mistress' scarf.

SILVIO.   Yes, he protests
   He would do much for that taffeta –   25

DELIO. I think he would run away from a battle
   To save it from taking prisoner.

SILVIO.   He is horribly afraid
   Gunpowder will spoil the perfume on 't –

DELIO. I saw a Dutchman break his pate once
   For calling him pot-gun; he made his head   30
   Have a bore in 't, like a musket.

SILVIO. I would he had made a touch-hole to 't.
   He is indeed a guarded sumpter cloth,
   Only for the remove of the court.

   Enter BOSOLA.

PESCARA. Bosola arriv'd! what should be the business?   35
   Some falling out amongst the cardinals.
   These factions amongst great men, they are like
   Foxes: when their heads are divided
   They carry fire in their tails, and all the country
   About them goes to wreck for 't.

SILVIO.   What's that Bosola?   40

DELIO. I knew him in Padua – a fantastical scholar, like such
   who study to know how many knots was in Hercules' club, of
   what colour Achilles' beard was, or whether Hector were not
   troubled with the toothache; he hath studied himself half
   blear-eyed to know the true symmetry of Caesar's nose   45
   by a shoeing-horn; and this he did to gain the name of a
   speculative man.

PESCARA. Mark Prince Ferdinand:
   A very salamander lives in's eye,
   To mock the eager violence of fire.   50

SILVIO. That cardinal hath made more bad faces with his
   oppression than ever Michael Angelo made good ones; he

lifts up's nose, like a foul porpoise before a storm –

PESCARA. The Lord Ferdinand laughs.

DELIO.   Like a deadly cannon
  That lightens ere it smokes.   55

PESCARA. These are your true pangs of death,
  The pangs of life that struggle with great statesmen –

DELIO. In such a deformed silence, witches whisper
  Their charms.

CARDINAL. Doth she make religion her riding-hood   60
  To keep her from the sun and tempest?

FERDINAND.   That!
  That damns her: – methinks her fault and beauty,
  Blended together, show like leprosy,
  The whiter, the fouler: – I make it a question
  Whether her beggarly brats were ever christen'd.   65

CARDINAL. I will instantly solicit the state of Ancona
  To have them banish'd.

FERDINAND.   You are for Loretto?
  I shall not be at your ceremony: fare you well –
  Write to the Duke of Malfi, my young nephew
  She had by her first husband, and acquaint him   70
  With 's mother's honesty.

BOSOLA.   I will.

FERDINAND.   Antonio!
  A slave, that only smell'd of ink and counters,
  And ne'er in's life look'd like a gentleman,
  But in the audit-time – go, go presently,
  Draw me out an hundred and fifty of our horse,   75
  And meet me at the fort-bridge.

Exeunt.

Act Three, Scene Four

Enter TWO PILGRIMS *to the Shrine of our Lady of Loretto.*

FIRST PILGRIM. I have not seen a goodlier shrine than this,
Yet I have visited many.

SECOND PILGRIM. The Cardinal of Arragon
Is this day to resign his cardinal's hat;
His sister duchess likewise is arriv'd
To pay her vow of pilgrimage – I expect
A noble ceremony.

FIRST PILGRIM. No question: – they come.

Here the ceremony of the CARDINAL*'s instalment in the habit of a soldier, performed in delivering up his cross, hat, robes and ring at the shrine, and investing him with sword, helmet, shield and spurs; then* ANTONIO, *the* DUCHESS *and their* CHILDREN, *having presented themselves at the shrine, are (by a form of banishment in dumb-show expressed towards them by the cardinal and the state of Ancona) banished: during all which ceremony, this ditty is sung, to very solemn music, by divers* CHURCHMEN; *and then exeunt [all, except the* TWO PILGRIMS].

Arms and honours deck thy story
To thy fame's eternal glory!
Adverse fortune ever fly thee,
No disastrous fate come nigh thee!

The author disclaims this ditty to be his.

I alone will sing thy praises,
Whom to honour virtue raises,
And thy study, that divine is,
Bent to martial discipline is:
Lay aside all those robes lie by thee;
Crown thy arts with arms, they'll beautify thee.

O worthy of worthiest name, adorn'd in this manner,
Lead bravely thy forces on under war's warlike banner!
O, mayst thou prove fortunate in all martial courses!
Guide thou still, by skill, in arts and forces!
Victory attend thee nigh whilst Fame sings loud thy pow'rs;
Triumphant conquest crown thy head, and blessings pour down show'rs!

FIRST PILGRIM. Here's a strange turn of state! who would have
     thought
  So great a lady would have match'd herself   25
  Unto so mean a person? yet the cardinal
  Bears himself much too cruel.

SECOND PILGRIM.   They are banish'd.

FIRST PILGRIM. But I would ask what power hath this state
  Of Ancona to determine of a free prince?

SECOND PILGRIM. They are a free state sir, and her brother
     show'd   30
  How that the Pope, fore-hearing of her looseness,
  Hath seiz'd into th' protection of the church
  The dukedom, which she held as dowager.

FIRST PILGRIM. But by what justice?

SECOND PILGRIM.   Sure, I think by none,
  Only her brother's instigation.   35

FIRST PILGRIM. What was it with such violence he took
  Off from her finger?

SECOND PILGRIM.   'Twas her wedding ring,
  Which he vow'd shortly he would sacrifice
  To his revenge.

FIRST PILGRIM.   Alas, Antonio!
  If that a man be thrust into a well,   40
  No matter who sets hand to 't, his own weight
  Will bring him sooner to th' bottom: – come, let's hence.
  Fortune makes this conclusion general:
  All things do help th' unhappy man to fall.

  Exeunt.

Act Three Scene Five

Enter ANTONIO, DUCHESS, CHILDREN, CARIOLA,
SERVANTS.

DUCHESS. Banish'd Ancona!

ANTONIO.   Yes, you see what pow'r
  Lightens in great men's breath.

DUCHESS.   Is all our train
  Shrunk to this poor remainder?

ANTONIO.   These poor men,
  Which have got little in your service, vow
  To take your fortune: but your wiser buntings,   5
  Now they are fledg'd, are gone.

DUCHESS.   They have done wisely –
  This puts me in mind of death: physicians thus,
  With their hands full of money, use to give o'er
  Their patients.

ANTONIO.   Right the fashion of the world:
  From decay'd fortunes every flatterer shrinks;   10
  Men cease to build where the foundation sinks.

DUCHESS. I had a very strange dream tonight.

ANTONIO.   What was 't?

DUCHESS. Methought I wore my coronet of state,
  And on a sudden all the diamonds
  Were chang'd to pearls.

ANTONIO.   My interpretation   15
  Is, you'll weep shortly, for to me, the pearls
  Do signify your tears: –

DUCHESS. The birds that live i' th' field
  On the wild benefit of nature, live
  Happier than we; for they may choose their mates,   20
  And carol their sweet pleasures to the spring: –

Enter BOSOLA [*with a letter*].

BOSOLA. You are happily o'erta'en.

DUCHESS.   From my brother?

BOSOLA. Yes, from the Lord Ferdinand, your brother,
    All love and safety –

DUCHESS.   Thou dost blanch mischief,
    Wouldst make it white: – see, see, like to calm weather   25
    At sea, before a tempest, false hearts speak fair
    To those they intend most mischief.
    (*Reads.*) *Send Antonio to me; I want his head in a business:* –
    A politic equivocation!
    He doth not want your counsel, but your head;   30
    That is, he cannot sleep till you be dead.
    And here's another pitfall, that's strew'd o'er
    With roses; mark it, 'tis a cunning one:
    [*Reads.*] *I stand engaged for your husband, for several debts*
    at Naples: let not that trouble him, I had rather have his heart than   35
    his money.
    And I believe so too.

BOSOLA.   What do you believe?

DUCHESS. That he so much distrusts my husband's love,
    He will by no means believe his heart is with him
    Until he see it: the devil is not cunning enough   40
    To circumvent us in riddles.

BOSOLA. Will you reject that noble and free league
    Of amity and love which I present you?

DUCHESS. Their league is like that of some politic kings,
    Only to make themselves of strength and pow'r   45
    To be our after-ruin: tell them so.

BOSOLA. And what from you?

ANTONIO.   Thus tell him: I will not come.

BOSOLA. And what of this?

ANTONIO.   My brothers have dispers'd
    Bloodhounds abroad; which till I hear are muzzled,

No truce, though hatch'd with ne'er such politic skill   50
Is safe, that hangs upon our enemies' will.
I'll not come at them.

BOSOLA.   This proclaims your breeding.
Every small thing draws a base mind to fear,
As the adamant draws iron; fare you well sir,
You shall shortly hear from 's.   55

Exit.

DUCHESS. I suspect some ambush:
Therefore by all my love, I do conjure you
To take your eldest son, and fly towards Milan:
Let us not venture all this poor remainder
In one unlucky bottom.

ANTONIO.   You counsel safely: –   60
Best of my life, farewell: since we must part·
Heaven hath a hand in 't; but no otherwise
Than as some curious artist takes in sunder
A clock or watch when it is out of frame,
To bring 't in better order.   65

DUCHESS. I know not which is best,
To see you dead, or part with you: – farewell boy;
Thou art happy, that thou hast not understanding
To know thy misery, for all our wit
And reading brings us to a truer sense   70
Of sorrow: – in the eternal church, sir,
I do hope we shall not part thus.

ANTONIO.   O, be of comfort!
Make patience a noble fortitude,
And think not how unkindly we are us'd:
Man, like to cassia, is prov'd best, being bruis'd.   75

DUCHESS. Must I, like to a slave-born Russian,
Account it praise to suffer tyranny?
And yet, O Heaven, thy heavy hand is in 't.
I have seen my little boy oft scourge his top
And compar'd myself to 't: naught made me e'er   80

Go right but heaven's scourge-stick.

ANTONIO.   Do not weep:
  Heaven fashion'd us of nothing; and we strive
  To bring ourselves to nothing: – farewell Cariola,
  And thy sweet armful: if I do never see thee more,
  Be a good mother to your little ones,   85
  And save them from the tiger: fare you well.

DUCHESS. Let me look upon you once more; for that speech
  Came from a dying father: your kiss is colder
  Than that I have seen an holy anchorite
  Give to a dead man's skull.   90

ANTONIO. My heart is turn'd to a heavy lump of lead,
  With which I sound my danger: fare you well.

  Exit [, with his elder SON].

DUCHESS. My laurel is all withered.

CARIOLA. Look, madam, what a troop of armed men
  Make toward us.

  Enter BOSOLA *with a* GUARD, *with visards*

DUCHESS.   O, they are very welcome: 95
  When Fortune's wheel is overcharg'd with princes,
  The weight makes it move swift. I would have my ruin
  Be sudden: – I am your adventure, am I not?

BOSOLA. You are, you must see your husband no more –   99

DUCHESS. What devil art thou, that counterfeits heaven's thunder?

BOSOLA. Is that terrible? I would have you tell me
  Whether is that note worse that frights the silly birds
  Out of the corn, or that which doth allure them
  To the nets? you have hearken'd to the last too much.

DUCHESS. O misery! like to a rusty o'ercharg'd cannon,   105
  Shall I never fly in pieces? come: to what prison?

BOSOLA. To none: –

DUCHESS.   Whither then?

BOSOLA. To your palace.

DUCHESS. I have heard
That Charon's boat serves to convey all o'er
The dismal lake, but brings none back again.

BOSOLA. Your brothers mean you safety, and pity.

DUCHESS. Pity! 110
With such a pity men preserve alive
Pheasants and quails, when they are not fat enough
To be eaten.

BOSOLA. These are your children?

DUCHESS. Yes: –

BOSOLA. Can they prattle?

DUCHESS. No:
But I intend, since they were born accurs'd, 115
Curses shall be their first language.

BOSOLA. Fie, madam,
Forget this base, low fellow.

DUCHESS. Were I a man
I'd beat that counterfeit face into thy other.

BOSOLA. One of no birth –

DUCHESS. Say that he was born mean:
Man is most happy when 's own actions 120
Be arguments and examples of his virtue.

BOSOLA. A barren, beggarly virtue.

DUCHESS. I prithee, who is greatest? can you tell?
Sad tales befit my woe: I'll tell you one.
A salmon, as she swam unto the sea, 125
Met with a dog-fish, who encounters her
With this rough language: 'Why art thou so bold
To mix thyself with our high state of floods,
Being no eminent courtier, but one
That for the calmest and fresh time o' th' year 130

Dost live in shallow rivers, rank'st thyself
With silly smelts and shrimps? and darest thou
Pass by our dog-ship, without reverence?'
'O', quoth the salmon, 'sister, be at peace:
Thank Jupiter we both have pass'd the net!   135
Our value never can be truly known
Till in the fisher's basket we be shown;
I' th' market then my price may be the higher,
Even when I am nearest to the cook and fire.'
So, to great men, the moral may be stretched: 140
Men oft are valued high, when th' are most wretched.
But come; whither you please: I am arm'd 'gainst misery;
Bent to all sways of the oppressor's will.
There's no deep valley, but near some great hill.

Exeunt.

Act Four, Scene One

Enter FERDINAND *and* BOSOLA.

FERDINAND. How doth our sister duchess bear herself
   In her imprisonment?

BOSOLA.   Nobly; I'll describe her:
   She's sad, as one long us'd to 't; and she seems
   Rather to welcome the end of misery
   Than shun it: – a behaviour so noble   5
   As gives a majesty to adversity;
   You may discern the shape of loveliness
   More perfect in her tears, than in her smiles;
   She will muse four hours together, and her silence,
   Methinks, expresseth more than if she spake.   10

FERDINAND. Her melancholy seems to be fortify'd
   With a strange disdain.

BOSOLA.   'Tis so: and this restraint
   (Like English mastiffs, that grow fierce with tying)
   Makes her too passionately apprehend
   Those pleasures she's kept from.

FERDINAND.   Curse upon her!   15
   I will no longer study in the book
   Of another's heart: inform her what I told you.

   Exit. Enter DUCHESS.

BOSOLA. All comfort to your grace!

DUCHESS.   I will have none: –
   Pray thee, why dost thou wrap thy poison'd pills
   In gold and sugar?   20

BOSOLA. Your elder brother, the Lord Ferdinand,
    Is come to visit you: and sends you word,
    'Cause once he rashly made a solemn vow
    Never to see you more, he comes i' th' night;
    And prays you, gently, neither torch nor taper   25
    Shine in your chamber: he will kiss your hand,
    And reconcile himself; but, for his vow,
    He dares not see you: –

DUCHESS.   At his pleasure;
    Take hence the lights:

    [BOSOLA *removes lights. Enter* FERDINAND.]

                          he's come.

FERDINAND.   Where are you?

DUCHESS.   Here sir: –

FERDINAND. This darkness suits you well.   30

DUCHESS. I would ask you pardon: –

FERDINAND.   You have it;
    For I account it the honourabl'st revenge,
    Where I may kill, to pardon: – where are your cubs?

DUCHESS. Whom?

FERDINAND. Call them your children;   35
    For though our national law distinguish bastards
    From true legitimate issue, compassionate nature
    Makes them all equal.

DUCHESS.   Do you visit me for this?
    You violate a sacrament o' th' church
    Shall make you howl in hell for 't.

FERDINAND. It had been well   40
    Could you have liv'd thus always; for indeed
    You were too much i' th' light: – but no more –
    I come to seal my peace with you: here's a hand

    Gives her a dead man's hand.

To which you have vow'd much love; the ring upon 't
You gave.

DUCHESS. I affectionately kiss it.   45

FERDINAND. Pray do: and bury the print of it in your heart:
I will leave this ring with you for a love-token;
And the hand, as sure as the ring; and do not doubt
But you shall have the heart too; when you need a friend
Send it to him that ow'd it; you shall see   50
Whether he can aid you.

DUCHESS.   You are very cold.
I fear you are not well after your travel: –
Hah! lights! – O, horrible!

FERDINAND. Let her have lights enough.

Exit.

DUCHESS. What witchcraft doth he practise that he hath left
A dead man's hand here? –   55

*Here is discovered, behind a traverse, the artificial figures of Antonio and
his children, appearing as if they were dead.*

BOSOLA. Look you: here's the piece from which 'twas ta'en:
He doth present you this sad spectacle
That now you know directly they are dead –
Hereafter you may wisely cease to grieve
For that which cannot be recovered.   60

DUCHESS. There is not between heaven and earth one wish
I stay for after this: it wastes me more
Than were 't my picture, fashion'd out of wax,
Stuck with a magical needle and then buried
In some foul dunghill; and yon's an excellent property   65
For a tyrant, which I would account mercy.

BOSOLA. What's that?

DUCHESS. If they would bind me to that lifeless trunk,
And let me freeze to death.

BOSOLA.   Come, you must live.

DUCHESS. That's the greatest torture souls feel in hell –   70
    In hell: that they must live, and cannot die.
    Portia, I'll new-kindle thy coals again,
    And revive the rare and almost dead example
    Of a loving wife.

BOSOLA.   O fie! despair? remember
    You are a Christian.

DUCHESS.   The church enjoins fasting :   75
    I'll starve myself to death.

BOSOLA.   Leave this vain sorrow:
    Things being at the worst begin to mend;
    The bee when he hath shot his sting into your hand
    May then play with your eyelid.

DUCHESS. Good comfortable fellow   80
    Persuade a wretch that's broke upon the wheel
    To have all his bones new set; entreat him live
    To be executed again: – who must despatch me?
    I account this world a tedious theatre,
    For I do play a part in 't 'gainst my will.   85

BOSOLA. Come, be of comfort, I will save your life.

DUCHESS. Indeed I have not leisure to tend so small a business.

BOSOLA. Now, by my life, I pity you.

DUCHESS.   Thou art a fool then,
    To waste thy pity on a thing so wretch'd
    As cannot pity itself: – I am full of daggers: 90
    Puff: let me blow these vipers from me.

    Enter SERVANT.

    What are you?

SERVANT.   One that wishes you long life.

DUCHESS. I would thou wert hang'd for the horrible curse
    Thou hast given me:

[*Exit* SERVANT.]

                  I shall shortly grow one
Of the miracles of pity: – I'll go pray: no,   95
I'll go curse: –

BOSOLA.   O fie!

DUCHESS.   I could curse the stars.

BOSOLA.   O fearful!

DUCHESS. And those three smiling seasons of the year
    Into a Russian winter, nay the world
    To its first chaos.

BOSOLA. Look you, the stars shine still: –

DUCHESS.   O, but you must   100
    Remember, my curse hath a great way to go. –
    Plagues, that make lanes through largest families,
    Consume them! –

BOSOLA.   Fie lady!

DUCHESS.   Let them, like tyrants,
    Never be remember'd, but for the ill they have done;
    Let all the zealous prayers of mortified   105
    Churchmen forget them! –

BOSOLA.   O, uncharitable!

DUCHESS. Let heaven, a little while, cease crowning martyrs,
    To punish them!
    Go howl them this: and say I long to bleed:
    It is some mercy, when men kill with speed.   110

    Exit. [*Enter* FERDINAND.]

FERDINAND. Excellent: as I would wish; she's plagu'd in art.
    These presentations are but fram'd in wax,
    By the curious master in that quality,
    Vincentio Lauriola, and she takes them
    For true substantial bodies.   115

BOSOLA. Why do you do this?

FERDINAND.   To bring her to despair.

BOSOLA. Faith, end here:
    And go no farther in your cruelty –
    Send her a penitential garment to put on
    Next to her delicate skin, and furnish her   120
    With beads and prayer-books.

FERDINAND. Damn her! that body of hers,
    While that my blood ran pure in 't, was more worth
    Than that which thou wouldst comfort, call'd a soul –
    I will send her masques of common courtesans,
    Have her meat serv'd up by bawds and ruffians,   125
    And, 'cause she'll needs be mad, I am resolv'd
    To remove forth the common hospital
    All the mad-folk, and place them near her lodging;
    There let them practise together, sing, and dance,
    And act their gambols to the full o' th' moon: 130
    If she can sleep the better for it, let her –
    Your work is almost ended.

BOSOLA. Must I see her again?

FERDINAND.   Yes.

BOSOLA.   Never.

FERDINAND.   You must.

BOSOLA. Never in mine own shape,
    That's forfeited by my intelligence,   135
    And this last cruel lie: when you send me next,
    The business shall be comfort.

FERDINAND.   Very likely –
    Thy pity is nothing of kin to thee: – Antonio
    Lurks about Milan; thou shalt shortly thither
    To feed a fire, as great as my revenge,   140
    Which ne'er will slack, till it have spent his fuel:
    Intemperate agues make physicians cruel.

    Exeunt.

Act Four, Scene Two

Enter DUCHESS *and* CARIOLA.

DUCHESS. What hideous noise was that?

CARIOLA.   'Tis the wild consort
    Of madmen, lady, which your tyrant brother
    Hath plac'd about your lodging: – this tyranny,
    I think, was never practis'd till this hour.

DUCHESS. Indeed I thank him: nothing but noise and folly   5
    Can keep me in my right wits, whereas reason
    And silence make me stark mad: – sit down;
    Discourse to me some dismal tragedy.

CARIOLA. O, 'twill increase your melancholy.

DUCHESS.   Thou art deceiv'd,
    To hear of greater grief would lessen mine –   10
    This is a prison?

CARIOLA.   Yes, but you shall live
    To shake this durance off.

DUCHESS.   Thou art a fool;
    The robin-redbreast, and the nightingale,
    Never live long in cages.

CARIOLA.   Pray dry your eyes.
    What think you of, madam?

DUCHESS.   Of nothing: 15
    When I muse thus, I sleep.

CARIOLA. Like a madman, with your eyes open?

DUCHESS. Dost thou think we shall know one another,
    In th' other world?

CARIOLA.   Yes, out of question.

DUCHESS. O that it were possible we might   20
    But hold some two days' conference with the dead,
    From them I should learn somewhat, I am sure
    I never shall know here: – I'll tell thee a miracle –

I am not mad yet, to my cause of sorrow.
Th' heaven o'er my head seems made of molten brass,   25
The earth of flaming sulphur, yet I am not mad:
I am acquainted with sad misery,
As the tann'd galley-slave is with his oar;
Necessity makes me suffer constantly,
And custom makes it easy – who do I look like now?   30

CARIOLA. Like to your picture in the gallery,
A deal of life in show, but none in practice;
Or rather like some reverend monument
Whose ruins are even pitied.

DUCHESS.   Very proper:
And Fortune seems only to have her eyesight   35
To behold my tragedy: – How now!
What noise is that?

Enter SERVANT.

SERVANT.   I am come to tell you
Your brother hath intended you some sport:
A great physician, when the Pope was sick
Of a deep melancholy, presented him   40
With several sorts of madmen, which wild object,
Being full of change and sport, forc'd him to laugh,
And so th' imposthume broke: the self-same cure
The duke intends on you.

DUCHESS.   Let them come in.

SERVANT. There's a mad lawyer, and a secular priest,   45
A doctor that hath forfeited his wits
By jealousy; an astrologian
That in his works said such a day o' th' month
Should be the day of doom, and failing of 't,
Ran mad; an English tailor, craz'd i' th' brain   50
With the study of new fashion; a gentleman usher
Quite beside himself, with care to keep in mind
The number of his lady's salutations,
Or 'How do you', she employ'd him in each morning;

A farmer too, an excellent knave in grain,   55
Mad 'cause he was hinder'd transportation:
And let one broker that's mad loose to these,
You'd think the devil were among them.

DUCHESS. Sit Cariola: let them loose when you please,
For I am chain'd to endure all your tyranny.   60

Enter MADMEN.

Here, by a MADMAN, *this song is sung, to a dismal kind of music.*

O, let us howl, some heavy note,
*   Some deadly dogged howl,*
Sounding as from the threat'ning throat
*   Of beasts, and fatal fowl!*
As ravens, screech-owls, bulls, and bears,   65
*   We'll bill and bawl our parts,*
Till irksome noise have cloy'd your ears
*   And corrosiv'd your hearts.*
At last when as our choir wants breath,
*   Our bodies being blest,*   70
We'll sing like swans, to welcome death,
*   And die in love and rest.*

FIRST MADMAN. Doomsday not come yet? I'll draw it nearer
by a perspective, or make a glass that shall set all the
world on fire upon an instant: I cannot sleep; my pillow   75
is stuffed with a litter of porcupines.

SECOND MADMAN. Hell is a mere glass-house, where the devils
are continually blowing up women's souls, on hollow irons,
and the fire never goes out.

THIRD MADMAN. I will lie with every woman in my parish   80
the tenth night: I will tythe them over, like hay-cocks.

FOURTH MADMAN. Shall my pothecary outgo me, because
I am a cuckold? I have found out his roguery: he makes alum
of his wife's urine, and sells it to puritans that have sore
throats with over-straining.   85

FIRST MADMAN. I have skill in heraldry.

SECOND MADMAN. Hast?

FIRST MADMAN. You do give for your crest a woodcock's
    head, with the brains picked out on 't – you are a very ancient
    gentleman.   90

THIRD MADMAN. Greek is turned Turk; we are only to be
    saved by the Helvetian translation.

FIRST MADMAN. Come on sir, I will lay the law to you.

SECOND MADMAN. O, rather lay a corrosive; the law will
    eat to the bone.   95

THIRD MADMAN. He that drinks but to satisfy nature is
    damned.

FOURTH MADMAN. If I had my glass here, I would show a
    sight should make all the women here call me mad doctor.

FIRST MADMAN. What's he, a rope-maker? [*Points at* THIRD
    MADMAN.]   100

SECOND MADMAN. No, no, no, a snuffling knave, that
    while he shows the tombs, will have his hand in a wench's
    placket.

THIRD MADMAN. Woe to the caroche, that brought home
    my wife from the masque, at three o'clock in the morning!   105
    it had a large featherbed in it.

FOURTH MADMAN. I have pared the devil's nails forty
    times, roasted them in raven's eggs, and cured agues with
    them.

THIRD MADMAN. Get me three hundred milch-bats to make   110
    possets, to procure sleep.

FOURTH MADMAN. All the college may throw their caps at
    me, I have made a soap-boiler costive – it was my master-
    piece: –

Here the dance, consisting of EIGHT MADMEN, *with music answer-*
able thereunto; after which BOSOLA, *like an old man, enters* [*and the*
MADMEN *leave*].

DUCHESS. Is he mad too?

SERVANT.   Pray question him: I'll leave you.   115

   [*Exit.*]

BOSOLA. I am come to make thy tomb.

DUCHESS.   Hah, my tomb!
   Thou speak'st as if I lay upon my death-bed,
   Gasping for breath: dost thou perceive me sick?

BOSOLA. Yes, and the more dangerously, since thy sickness is
   insensible.   120

DUCHESS. Thou art not mad, sure – dost know me?

BOSOLA. Yes.

DUCHESS. Who am I?

BOSOLA. Thou art a box of worm-seed, at best, but a
   salvatory of green mummy: – what's this flesh? a little   125
   crudded milk, fantastical puff-paste; our bodies are weaker
   than those paper prisons boys use to keep flies in; more
   contemptible, since ours is to preserve earth-worms.
   Didst thou ever see a lark in a cage? such is the soul
   in the body: this world is like her little turf of grass, and   130
   the heaven o'er our heads, like her looking-glass, only
   gives us a miserable knowledge of the small compass of
   our prison.

DUCHESS. Am not I thy duchess?

BOSOLA. Thou art some great woman, sure, for riot begins   135
   to sit on thy forehead, clad in gray hairs, twenty years sooner
   than on a merry milkmaid's. Thou sleepest worse than
   if a mouse should be forced to take up her lodging in a
   cat's ear: a little infant that breeds its teeth, should it lie
   with thee, would cry out, as if thou wert the more unquiet   140
   bedfellow.

DUCHESS. I am Duchess of Malfi still.

BOSOLA. That makes thy sleeps so broken:

Glories, like glow-worms, afar off shine bright,
But look'd to near, have neither heat, nor light.   145

DUCHESS. Thou art very plain.

BOSOLA. My trade is to flatter the dead, not the living – I am a
tomb-maker.

DUCHESS. And thou comest to make my tomb?

BOSOLA. Yes.   150

DUCHESS. Let me be a little merry – of what stuff wilt thou
make it?

BOSOLA. Nay, resolve me first, of what fashion?

DUCHESS. Why, do we grow fantastical in our death-bed? do
we affect fashion in the grave?   155

BOSOLA. Most ambitiously: princes' images on their tombs
do not lie, as they were wont, seeming to pray up to heaven,
but with their hands under their cheeks, as if they died of
the tooth-ache; they are not carved with their eyes fixed
upon the stars, but as their minds were wholly bent upon   160
the world, the selfsame way they seem to turn their
faces.

DUCHESS. Let me know fully therefore the effect
Of this thy dismal preparation,
This talk fit for a charnel.

BOSOLA.   Now I shall: 165

Enter EXECUTIONERS[*, with*] *a coffin, cords and a bell.*

Here is a present from your princely brothers,
And may it arrive welcome, for it brings
Last benefit, last sorrow.

DUCHESS.   Let me see it –
I have so much obedience in my blood,
I wish it in their veins, to do them good.   170

BOSOLA. This is your last presence-chamber.

CARIOLA. O my sweet lady!

DUCHESS.   Peace, it affrights not me.

BOSOLA. I am the common bellman
    That usually is sent to condemn'd persons
    The night before they suffer: –

DUCHESS.   Even now thou said'st   175
    Thou wast a tomb-maker.

BOSOLA.   'Twas to bring you
    By degrees to mortification. Listen:

> *Hark, now everything is still,*
> *The screech-owl, and the whistler shrill*
> *Call upon our dame, aloud,*   178 180
> *And bid her quickly don her shroud.*
> *Much you had of land and rent,*
> *Your length in clay's now competent.*
> *A long war disturb'd your mind*
> *Here your perfect peace is sign'd.*   185
> *Of what is' t fools make such vain keeping?*
> *Sin their conception, their birth weeping;*
> *Their life a general mist of error,*
> *Their death a hideous storm of terror.*
> *Strew your hair with powders sweet,*   190
> *Don clean linen, bathe your feet,*
> *And (the foul fiend more to check)*
> *A crucifix let bless your neck.*
> *'Tis now full tide, 'tween night and day:*
> *End your groan, and come away.*   195

CARIOLA. Hence villains, tyrants, murderers! alas!
    What will you do with my lady? call for help.

DUCHESS. To whom? to our next neighbours? they are mad-folks.

BOSOLA. Remove that noise.

DUCHESS.   Farewell Cariola:
    In my last will I have not much to give;   200
    A many hungry guests have fed upon me,

Thine will be a poor reversion.

CARIOLA.   I will die with her.

DUCHESS. I pray thee, look thou giv'st my little boy
    Some syrup for his cold, and let the girl
    Say her prayers, ere she sleep.

    [EXECUTIONERS *force* CARIOLA *off.*]

                        Now what you please –   205
    What death?

BOSOLA.   Strangling: here are your executioners.

DUCHESS. I forgive them:
    The apoplexy, catarrh, or cough o' th' lungs
    Would do as much as they do.   209

BOSOLA. Doth not death fright you?

DUCHESS.   Who would be afraid on 't?
    Knowing to meet such excellent company
    In th' other world.

BOSOLA.   Yet, methinks,
    The manner of your death should much afflict you,
    This cord should terrify you?

DUCHESS.   Not a whit: 215
    What would it pleasure me to have my throat cut
    With diamonds? or to be smothered
    With cassia? or to be shot to death with pearls?
    I know death hath ten thousand several doors
    For men to take their exits; and 'tis found   220
    They go on such strange geometrical hinges,
    You may open them both ways: – any way, for heaven-sake,
    So I were out of your whispering: – tell my brothers
    That I perceive death, now I am well awake,
    Best gift is they can give, or I can take.   225
    I would fain put off my last woman's fault,
    I'd not be tedious to you.

EXECUTIONERS.   We are ready.

DUCHESS. Dispose my breath how please you, but my body
    Bestow upon my women, will you?

EXECUTIONERS.   Yes.

DUCHESS. Pull, and pull strongly, for your able strength   230
    Must pull down heaven upon me: –
    Yet stay; heaven-gates are not so highly arch'd
    As princes' palaces, they that enter there
    Must go upon their knees. – [*Kneels.*] Come violent death,
    Serve for mandragora to make me sleep!   235
    Go tell my brothers, when I am laid out,
    They then may feed in quiet.

They strangle her.

BOSOLA. Where's the waiting woman?
    Fetch her: some other strangle the children.

[EXECUTIONERS *fetch* CARIOLA, *and one goes to strangle the children.*]

    Look you, there sleeps your mistress.

CARIOLA.   O, you are damn'd   240
    Perpetually for this: – my turn is next,
    Is' t not so order'd?

BOSOLA.   Yes, and I am glad
    You are so well prepar'd for 't.

CARIOLA.   You are deceiv'd sir,
    I am not prepar'd for 't, I will not die;
    I will first come to my answer, and know   245
    How I have offended.

BOSOLA.   Come, despatch her: –
    You kept her counsel, now you shall keep ours.

CARIOLA. I will not die, I must not, I am contracted
    To a young gentleman.

EXECUTIONER.   Here's your wedding ring.

CARIOLA. Let me but speak with the duke: I'll discover   250

Treason to his person.

BOSOLA.   Delays: – throttle her.

EXECUTIONER. She bites, and scratches: –

CARIOLA.   If you kill me now
I am damn'd: I have not been at confession
This two years: –

BOSOLA.   When?

CARIOLA.   I am quick with child.

BOSOLA.   Why then,
Your credit's sav'd: –

[*The* EXECUTIONERS *strangle* CARIOLA.]

                    bear her into th' next room;   255
Let this lie still.

[*Exeunt* EXECUTIONERS *with the body of* CARIOLA.]

Enter FERDINAND.

FERDINAND.   Is she dead?

BOSOLA.   She is what
You'd have her: but here begin your pity –

Shows the CHILDREN *strangled.*

Alas, how have these offended?

FERDINAND.   The death
Of young wolves is never to be pitied.

BOSOLA. Fix your eye here: –

FERDINAND.   Constantly.

BOSOLA.   Do you not weep?   260
Other sins only speak; murder shrieks out:
The element of water moistens the earth,
But blood flies upwards, and bedews the heavens.

FERDINAND. Cover her face: mine eyes dazzle: she died young.

BOSOLA. I think not so: her infelicity   265
    Seem'd to have years too many.

FERDINAND. She and I were twins:
    And should I die this instant, I had liv'd
    Her time to a minute.

BOSOLA.   It seems she was born first:
    You have bloodily approv'd the ancient truth,   270
    That kindred commonly do worse agree
    Than remote strangers.

FERDINAND.   Let me see her face again: –
    Why didst not thou pity her? what an excellent
    Honest man mightst thou have been
    If thou hadst borne her to some sanctuary!   275
    Or, bold in a good cause, oppos'd thyself
    With thy advanced sword above thy head,
    Between her innocence and my revenge!
    I bade thee, when I was distracted of my wits,
    Go kill my dearest friend, and thou hast done 't.   280
    For let me but examine well the cause:
    What was the meanness of her match to me?
    Only I must confess, I had a hope,
    Had she continu'd widow, to have gain'd
    An infinite mass of treasure by her death: 285
    And that was the main cause: . . . her marriage! –
    That drew a stream of gall, quite through my heart.
    For thee, (as we observe in tragedies
    That a good actor many times is curs'd
    For playing a villain's part) I hate thee for 't: 290
    And for my sake say thou hast done much ill well.

BOSOLA. Let me quicken your memory; for I perceive
    You are falling into ingratitude: I challenge
    The reward due to my service.

FERDINAND.   I'll tell thee
    What I'll give thee –

BOSOLA.   Do: –

FERDINAND.   I'll give thee a pardon   295
   For this murder: –

BOSOLA.   Hah?

FERDINAND.   Yes: and 'tis
   The largest bounty I can study to do thee.
   By what authority didst thou execute
   This bloody sentence?

BOSOLA.   By yours –

FERDINAND.   Mine? was I her judge?
   Did any ceremonial form of law   300
   Doom her to not-being? did a complete jury
   Deliver her conviction up i' th' court?
   Where shalt thou find this judgement register'd
   Unless in hell? See: like a bloody fool
   Th' hast forfeited thy life, and thou shalt die for 't.   305

BOSOLA. The office of justice is perverted quite
   When one thief hangs another: – who shall dare
   To reveal this?

FERDINAND.   O, I'll tell thee:
   The wolf shall find her grave, and scrape it up:
   Not to devour the corpse, but to discover   310
   The horrid murder.

BOSOLA.   You, not I, shall quake for 't

FERDINAND. Leave me: –

BOSOLA.   I will first receive my pension.

FERDINAND. You are a villain: –

BOSOLA.   When your ingratitude
   Is judge, I am so.

FERDINAND.   O horror!
   That not the fear of him which binds the devils   315
   Can prescribe man obedience!
   Never look upon me more.

BOSOLA.   Why fare thee well:
    Your brother and yourself are worthy men;
    You have a pair of hearts are hollow graves,
    Rotten, and rotting others: and your vengeance,   320
    Like two chain'd bullets, still goes arm in arm –
    You may be brothers; for treason, like the plague,
    Doth take much in a blood. I stand like one
    That long hath ta'en a sweet and golden dream:
    I am angry with myself, now that I wake.   325

FERDINAND. Get thee into some unknown part o' th' world
    That I may never see thee.

BOSOLA.   Let me know
    Wherefore I should be thus neglected? sir,
    I serv'd your tyranny; and rather strove
    To satisfy yourself, than all the world;   330
    And though I loath'd the evil, yet I lov'd
    You that did counsel it; and rather sought
    To appear a true servant, than an honest man.

FERDINAND. I'll go hunt the badger, by owl-light:
    'Tis a deed of darkness. (*Exit.*)   335

BOSOLA. He's much distracted: – off my painted honour:
    While with vain hopes our faculties we tire,
    We seem to sweat in ice, and freeze in fire.
    What would I do, were this to do again?
    I would not change my peace of conscience   340
    For all the wealth of Europe: – she stirs; here's life!
    Return, fair soul, from darkness, and lead mine
    Out of this sensible hell: – she's warm, she breathes: –
    Upon thy pale lips I will melt my heart
    To store them with fresh colour: – who's there?   345
    Some cordial drink! – Alas! I dare not call:
    So pity would destroy pity: – her eye opes,
    And heaven in it seems to ope, that late was shut,
    To take me up to mercy.

DUCHESS. Antonio!

BOSOLA.   Yes, madam, he is living –   350
  The dead bodies you saw were but feign'd statues;
  He's reconcil'd to your brothers; the Pope hath wrought
  The atonement.

DUCHESS.   Mercy!

She dies.

BOSOLA. O, she's gone again: there the cords of life broke.
  O sacred innocence, that sweetly sleeps   355
  On turtles' feathers, whilst a guilty conscience
  Is a black register, wherein is writ
  All our good deeds and bad, a perspective
  That shows us hell! That we cannot be suffer'd
  To do good when we have a mind to it!   360
  This is manly sorrow:
  These tears, I am very certain, never grew
  In my mother's milk. My estate is sunk
  Below the degree of fear: where were
  These penitent fountains while she was living?   365
  O, they were frozen up! Here is a sight
  As direful to my soul as is the sword
  Unto a wretch hath slain his father. Come,
  I'll bear thee hence:
  And execute thy last will; that's deliver   370
  Thy body to the reverent dispose
  Of some good women: that the cruel tyrant
  Shall not deny me. Then I'll post to Milan
  Where somewhat I will speedily enact
  Worth my dejection.

Exit [, with the body of the DUCHESS].

Act Five, Scene One

Enter ANTONIO *and* DELIO.

ANTONIO. What think you of my hope of reconcilement
    To the Arragonian brethren?

DELIO.   I misdoubt it,
    For though they have sent their letters of safe conduct
    For your repair to Milan, they appear
    But nets to entrap you: the Marquis of Pescara,   5
    Under whom you hold certain land in cheat,
    Much 'gainst his noble nature, hath been mov'd
    To seize those lands, and some of his dependants
    Are at this instant making it their suit
    To be invested in your revenues.   10
    I cannot think they mean well to your life
    That do deprive you of your means of life,
    Your living.

ANTONIO.   You are still an heretic
    To any safety I can shape myself.

Enter PESCARA.

DELIO. Here comes the Marquis: I will make myself   15
    Petitioner for some part of your land,
    To know whither it is flying.

ANTONIO.   I pray do. [*He retires.*]

DELIO. Sir, I have a suit to you.

PESCARA.   To me?

DELIO.   An easy one:
    There is the Citadel of Saint Bennet,
    With some demesnes, of late in the possession   20

Of Antonio Bologna – please you bestow them on me?

PESCARA. You are my friend: but this is such a suit,
    Nor fit for me to give, nor you to take.

DELIO. No sir?

PESCARA.   I will give you ample reason for 't
    Soon in private: –

Enter JULIA.

                        here's the cardinal's mistress.   25

JULIA. My lord, I am grown your poor petitioner,
    And should be an ill beggar, had I not
    A great man's letter here, the cardinal's,
    To court you in my favour. [*Gives letter.*]

PESCARA.   He entreats for you
    The Citadel of Saint Bennet, that belong'd   30
    To the banish'd Bologna.

JULIA.   Yes.

PESCARA. I could not have thought of a friend I could
    Rather pleasure with it: 'tis yours.

JULIA.   Sir, I thank you:
    And he shall know how doubly I am engag'd
    Both in your gift, and speediness of giving,   35
    Which makes your grant the greater.

    Exit.

ANTONIO [*aside*].   How they fortify
    Themselves with my ruin!

DELIO.   Sir, I am
    Little bound to you.

PESCARA.   Why?

DELIO. Because you deny'd this suit to me, and gave 't
    To such a creature.

PESCARA.   Do you know what it was?   40

It was Antonio's land: not forfeited
By course of law, but ravish'd from his throat
By the cardinal's entreaty: it were not fit
I should bestow so main a piece of wrong
Upon my friend; 'tis a gratification   45
Only due to a strumpet, for it is injustice.
Shall I sprinkle the pure blood of innocents
To make those followers I call my friends
Look ruddier upon me? I am glad
This land, ta'en from the owner by such wrong,   50
Returns again unto so foul an use
As salary for his lust. Learn, good Delio,
To ask noble things of me, and you shall find
I'll be a noble giver.

DELIO.   You instruct me well.   54

ANTONIO [aside]. Why, here's a man now, would fright impudence
    From sauciest beggars.

PESCARA. Prince Ferdinand's come to Milan
    Sick, as they give out, of an apoplexy;
    But some say 'tis a frenzy: I am going
    To visit him.

    Exit.

ANTONIO.   'Tis a noble old fellow. [*He advances.*]   60

DELIO. What course do you mean to take, Antonio?

ANTONIO. This night I mean to venture all my fortune
    (Which is no more than a poor ling'ring life)
    To the cardinal's worst of malice: I have got
    Private access to his chamber, and intend   65
    To visit him, about the mid of night,
    As once his brother did our noble duchess.
    It may be that the sudden apprehension
    Of danger – for I'll go in mine own shape –
    When he shall see it fraught with love and duty,   70
    May draw the poison out of him, and work
    A friendly reconcilement: if it fail,

Yet it shall rid me of this infamous calling;
For better fall once, than be ever falling.

DELIO. I'll second you in all danger: and how e'er,   75
    My life keeps rank with yours.

ANTONIO. You are still my lov'd, and best friend.

    Exeunt.

Act Five, Scene Two

Enter PESCARA *and a* DOCTOR.

PESCARA. Now doctor, may I visit your patient?

DOCTOR. If 't please your lordship: but he's instantly
    To take the air here in the gallery,
    By my direction.

PESCARA.   Pray thee, what's his disease?

DOCTOR. A very pestilent disease, my lord,   5
    They call lycanthropia.

PESCARA.   What's that?
    I need a dictionary to 't.

DOCTOR.   I'll tell you:
    In those that are possess'd with 't there o'erflows
    Such melancholy humour, they imagine
    Themselves to be transformed into wolves,   10
    Steal forth to churchyards in the dead of night,
    And dig dead bodies up: as two nights since
    One met the duke, 'bout midnight in a lane
    Behind Saint Mark's church, with the leg of a man
    Upon his shoulder; and he howl'd fearfully;   15
    Said he was a wolf, only the difference
    Was, a wolf's skin was hairy on the outside,

His on the inside; bade them take their swords,
Rip up his flesh, and try: straight I was sent for,
And having minister'd to him, found his grace   20
Very well recovered.

PESCARA.   I am glad on 't.

DOCTOR. Yet not without some fear
Of a relapse. If he grow to his fit again
I'll go a nearer way to work with him
Than ever Paracelsus dream'd of: if   25
They'll give me leave I'll buffet his madness out of him.

Enter FERDINAND, MALATESTE, *and* CARDINAL;
BOSOLA [*follows and watches, apart*].

Stand aside: he comes.

FERDINAND. Leave me.

MALATESTE. Why doth your lordship love this solitariness?

FERDINAND. Eagles commonly fly alone: they are crows,   30
daws, and starlings that flock together: – look, what's that
follows me?

MALATESTE. Nothing, my lord.

FERDINAND. Yes: –

MALATESTE. 'Tis your shadow .   35

FERDINAND. Stay it, let it not haunt me.

MALATESTE. Impossible: if you move, and the sun shine: –

FERDINAND. I will throttle it.

[*Throws himself down on his shadow.*]

MALATESTE. O, my lord: you are angry with nothing.

FERDINAND. You are a fool: how is' t possible I should catch   40
my shadow unless I fall upon 't? When I go to hell, I mean to
carry a bribe; for look you, good gifts evermore make way
for the worst persons.

PESCARA. Rise, good my lord.

FERDINAND. I am studying the art of patience.   45

PESCARA. 'Tis a noble virtue: –

FERDINAND. To drive six snails before me, from this town to
     Moscow; neither use goad nor whip to them, but let them
     take their own time: – the patientest man i' th' world match
     me for an experiment – and I'll crawl after like a sheep-   50
     biter.

CARDINAL. Force him up. [*They raise him.*]

FERDINAND. Use me well, you were best: what I have done, I have
     done: I'll confess nothing.

DOCTOR. Now let me come to him: – are you mad, my lord?   55
     are you out of your princely wits?

FERDINAND. What's he?

PESCARA. Your doctor.

FERDINAND. Let me have his beard sawed off, and his eyebrows
     filed more civil.   60

DOCTOR. I must do mad tricks with him, for that's the only
     way on 't. I have brought your grace a salamander's skin, to
     keep you from sun-burning.

FERDINAND. I have cruel sore eyes.

DOCTOR. The white of a cockatrix's egg is present remedy.   65

FERDINAND. Let it be a new-laid one, you were best: –

     Hide me from him; physicians are like kings,
     They brook no contradiction.

DOCTOR. Now he begins to fear me, now let me alone with him.

CARDINAL. How now, put off your gown!   70

DOCTOR. Let me have some forty urinals filled with rose-
     water: he and I'll go pelt one another with them – now he
     begins to fear me: – can you fetch a frisk, sir? – Let him

go, let him go upon my peril: I find by his eye, he stands
in awe of me; I'll make him as tame as a dormouse.   75

FERDINAND. Can you fetch your frisks, sir? – I will stamp
him into a cullis, flay off his skin, to cover one of the
anatomies this rogue hath set i' th' cold yonder, in Barber-
Chirurgeons' Hall. Hence, hence, you are all of you
like beasts for sacrifice; there's nothing left of you, but   80
tongue, and belly, flattery, and lechery. [*Exit.*]

PESCARA. Doctor, he did not fear you throughly.

DOCTOR. True, I was somewhat too forward. [*Exit.*]

BOSOLA. Mercy upon me, what a fatal judgement   85
Hath fall'n upon this Ferdinand!

PESCARA.   Knows your grace
What accident hath brought unto the prince
This strange distraction?

CARDINAL [*aside*]. I must feign somewhat: – [*To them.*] Thus they
      say it grew:
You have heard it rumour'd for these many years,   90
None of our family dies, but there is seen
The shape of an old woman, which is given
By tradition to us to have been murder'd
By her nephews, for her riches; such a figure
One night, as the prince sat up late at 's book,   95
Appear'd to him; when crying out for help,
The gentlemen of 's chamber found his grace
All on a cold sweat, alter'd much in face
And language; since which apparition,
He hath grown worse and worse, and I much fear   100
He cannot live.

BOSOLA.   Sir, I would speak with you.

PESCARA.   We'll leave your grace,
Wishing to the sick prince, our noble lord,
All health of mind and body.

CARDINAL.   You are most welcome.

[Exeunt all except CARDINAL *and* BOSOLA.]

[Aside.] Are you come? so: – this fellow must not know   105
By any means I had intelligence
In our duchess' death; for, though I counsell'd it,
The full of all th' engagement seem'd to grow
From Ferdinand. *[To him.]* Now sir, how fares our sister?
I do not think but sorrow makes her look   110
Like to an oft-dy'd garment: she shall now
Taste comfort from me – why do you look so wildly?
O, the fortune of your master here, the prince,
Dejects you – but be you of happy comfort:
If you'll do one thing for me I'll entreat,   115
Though he had a cold tomb-stone o'er his bones,
I'd make you what you would be.

BOSOLA.   Any thing –
Give it me in a breath, and let me fly to 't:
They that think long, small expedition win,
For musing much o' th' end, cannot begin.   120

Enter JULIA.

JULIA. Sir, will you come in to supper?

CARDINAL.   I am busy, leave me.

JULIA *[aside]*. What an excellent shape hath that fellow!

Exit.

CARDINAL. 'Tis thus: Antonio lurks here in Milan;
Inquire him out, and kill him: – while he lives
Our sister cannot marry, and I have thought   125
Of an excellent match for her: – do this, and style me
Thy advancement.

BOSOLA. But by what means shall I find him out?

CARDINAL. There is a gentleman, call'd Delio,
Here in the camp, that hath been long approv'd   130
His loyal friend: set eye upon that fellow,
Follow him to mass – may be Antonio,

Although he do account religion
But a school-name, for fashion of the world
May accompany him; or else go inquire out   135
Delio's confessor, and see if you can bribe
Him to reveal it; there are a thousand ways
A man might find to trace him; as to know
What fellows haunt the Jews for taking up
Great sums of money, for sure he's in want;   140
Or else to go to th' picture-makers and learn
Who bought her picture lately – some of these
Happily may take –

BOSOLA.   Well, I'll not freeze i' th' business;
I would see that wretched thing, Antonio,
Above all sights i' th' world.

CARDINAL.   Do, and be happy.   145

Exit.

BOSOLA. This fellow doth breed basilisks in 's eyes,
He's nothing else but murder: yet he seems
Not to have notice of the duchess' death –
'Tis his cunning: I must follow his example;
There cannot be a surer way to trace   150
Than that of an old fox.

[*Enter* JULIA *pointing a pistol at him.*]

JULIA.   So, sir, you are well met.

BOSOLA. How now?

JULIA.   Nay, the doors are fast enough: –
Now sir, I will make you confess your treachery.

BOSOLA. Treachery?

JULIA.   Yes, confess to me
Which of my women 'twas you hir'd, to put   155
Love-powder into my drink?

BOSOLA.   Love-powder!

JULIA.   Yes,

When I was at Malfi –
Why should I fall in love with such a face else?
I have already suffer'd for thee so much pain,
The only remedy to do me good   160
Is to kill my longing.

BOSOLA.   Sure your pistol holds
Nothing but perfumes, or kissing-comfits
Excellent lady,
You have a pretty way on 't to discover
Your longing: come, come, I'll disarm you,   165
And arm you thus – yet this is wondrous strange.

JULIA. Compare thy form, and my eyes together,
You'll find my love no such great miracle.
Now you'll say
I am wanton: this nice modesty in ladies   170
Is but a troublesome familiar
That haunts them.

BOSOLA. Know you me, I am a blunt soldier.

JULIA.   The better –
Sure, there wants fire where there are no lively sparks
Of roughness.

BOSOLA.   And I want compliment.

JULIA.   Why ignorance   175
In courtship cannot make you do amiss,
If you have a heart to do well.

BOSOLA.   You are very fair.

JULIA. Nay, if you lay beauty to my charge,
I must plead unguilty.

BOSOLA.   Your bright eyes
Carry a quiver of darts in them, sharper   180
Than sunbeams.

JULIA.   You will mar me with commendation,
Put yourself to the charge of courting me
Whereas now I woo you.

BOSOLA [*aside*]. I have it, I will work upon this creature –
   [*To her.*] Let us grow most amorously familiar: 185
   If the great cardinal now should see me thus,
   Would he not count me a villain?

JULIA. No: he might count me a wanton,
   Not lay a scruple of offence on you;
   For if I see and steal a diamond,   190
   The fault is not i' th' stone, but in me the thief
   That purloins it: – I am sudden with you;
   We that are great women of pleasure use to cut off
   These uncertain wishes, and unquiet longings,
   And in an instant join the sweet delight   195
   And the pretty excuse together; had you been i' th' street,
   Under my chamber window, even there
   I should have courted you.

BOSOLA.   O, you are an excellent lady.

JULIA. Bid me do somewhat for you presently,
   To express I love you.

BOSOLA.   I will, and if you love me,   200
   Fail not to effect it.
   The cardinal is grown wondrous melancholy;
   Demand the cause; let him not put you off
   With feign'd excuse, discover the main ground on 't.

JULIA. Why would you know this?

BOSOLA.   I have depended on him,   205
   And I hear that he is fall'n in some disgrace
   With the Emperor – if he be, like the mice
   That forsake falling houses, I would shift
   To other dependance.

JULIA. You shall not need follow the wars;   210
   I'll be your maintenance.

BOSOLA.   And I your loyal servant –
   But I cannot leave my calling.

JULIA.   Not leave

An ungrateful general, for the love of a sweet lady?
You are like some, cannot sleep in feather-beds,
But must have blocks for their pillows.

BOSOLA.   Will you do this?   215

JULIA. Cunningly.

BOSOLA.   Tomorrow I'll expect th' intelligence.

JULIA. Tomorrow? get you into my cabinet,
You shall have it with you: do not delay me,
No more than I do you; I am like one
That is condemn'd – I have my pardon promis'd,   220
But I would see it seal'd: – go, get you in,
You shall see me wind my tongue about his heart,
Like a skein of silk.

[*Exit* BOSOLA. *Enter* CARDINAL, *followed by* SERVANTS.]

CARDINAL. Where are you?

SERVANT.   Here.

CARDINAL.   Let none upon your lives
Have conference with the Prince Ferdinand,   225
Unless I know it: [*Exeunt* SERVANTS. *Aside*.] – in this distraction
He may reveal the murder.
Yon's my ling'ring consumption:
I am weary of her; and by any means
Would be quit of.

JULIA.   How now, my lord?   230
What ails you?

CARDINAL.   Nothing.

JULIA.   O, you are much alter'd:
Come, I must be your secretary, and remove
This lead from off your bosom – what's the matter?

CARDINAL. I may not tell you.

JULIA. Are you so far in love with sorrow,   235
You cannot part with part of it? or think you

I cannot love your grace when you are sad,
As well as merry? or do you suspect
I, that have been a secret to your heart
These many winters, cannot be the same   240
Unto your tongue?

CARDINAL.   Satisfy thy longing –
The only way to make thee keep my counsel
Is not to tell thee.

JULIA.   Tell your echo this,
Or flatterers that like echoes still report
What they hear though most imperfect, and not me: 245
For, if that you be true unto yourself,
I'll know.

CARDINAL. Will you rack me?

JULIA.   No, judgement shall
Draw it from you: it is an equal fault
To tell one's secrets unto all, or none.

CARDINAL. The first argues folly.

JULIA.   But the last tyranny.   250

CARDINAL. Very well – why imagine I have committed
Some secret deed, which I desire the world
May never hear of.

JULIA.   Therefore may not I know it?
You have conceal'd for me as great a sin
As adultery: – sir, never was occasion   255
For perfect trial of my constancy
Till now: sir, I beseech you.

CARDINAL.   You'll repent it.

JULIA.   Never.

CARDINAL. It hurries thee to ruin: I'll not tell thee –
Be well advis'd, and think what danger 'tis
To receive a prince's secrets: they that do,   260
Had need have their breasts hoop'd with adamant

To contain them: I pray thee yet be satisfy'd;
Examine thine own frailty; 'tis more easy
To tie knots, than unloose them: – 'tis a secret
That, like a ling'ring poison, may chance lie   265
Spread in thy veins, and kill thee seven year hence.

JULIA. Now you dally with me.

CARDINAL.   No more; thou shalt know it.
By my appointment, the great Duchess of Malfi,
And two of her young children, four nights since,
Were strangled.

JULIA.   O heaven! sir, what have you done?   270

CARDINAL. How now? how settles this? think you your bosom
Will be a grave, dark and obscure enough,
For such a secret?

JULIA.   You have undone yourself, sir.

CARDINAL. Why?

JULIA.   It lies not in me to conceal it.

CARDINAL.   No?
Come, I will swear you to 't upon this book.   275

JULIA. Most religiously.

CARDINAL.   Kiss it. [*She kisses the book.*]
Now you shall never utter it; thy curiosity
Hath undone thee: thou'rt poison'd with that book;
Because I knew thou couldst not keep my counsel,
I have bound thee to 't by death.   280

    [*Enter BOSOLA.*]

BOSOLA. For pity-sake, hold!

CARDINAL.   Ha, Bosola!

JULIA.   I forgive you –
This equal piece of justice you have done,
For I betray'd your counsel to that fellow:
He overheard it; that was the cause I said

It lay not in me to conceal it.   285

BOSOLA. O foolish woman,
    Couldst not thou have poison'd him?

JULIA.   'Tis weakness,
    Too much to think what should have been done – I go,
    I know not whither. [*Dies.*]

CARDINAL.   Wherefore com'st thou hither?

BOSOLA. That I might find a great man, like yourself,   290
    Not out of his wits as the Lord Ferdinand,
    To remember my service.

CARDINAL.   I'll have thee hew'd in pieces.

BOSOLA. Make not yourself such a promise of that life
    Which is not yours to dispose of.

CARDINAL.   Who plac'd thee here?

BOSOLA. Her lust, as she intended.

CARDINAL.   Very well,   295
    Now you know me for your fellow murderer.

BOSOLA. And wherefore should you lay fair marble colours
    Upon your rotten purposes to me?
    Unless you imitate some that do plot great treasons,
    And when they have done, go hide themselves i' th' graves   300
    Of those were actors in 't?

CARDINAL. No more, there is a fortune attends thee.

BOSOLA. Shall I go sue to Fortune any longer?
    'Tis the fool's pilgrimage.

CARDINAL.   I have honours in store for thee.

BOSOLA. There are a many ways that conduct to seeming   305
    Honour, and some of them very dirty ones.

CARDINAL. Throw to the devil
    Thy melancholy: the fire burns well,
    What need we keep a stirring of 't, and make

A greater smother? thou wilt kill Antonio?   310

BOSOLA. Yes.

CARDINAL.   Take up that body.

BOSOLA.   I think I shall
  Shortly grow the common bier for churchyards.

CARDINAL. I will allow thee some dozen of attendants
  To aid thee in the murder.

BOSOLA.   O, by no means:
  Physicians that apply horse-leeches to any rank swelling   315
  use to cut off their tails, that the blood may run through
  them the faster; let me have no train when I go to shed
  blood, lest it make me have a greater when I ride to the
  gallows.

CARDINAL. Come to me after midnight, to help to remove   320
  that body to her own lodging: I'll give out she died o' th'
  plague; 'twill breed the less inquiry after her death.

BOSOLA. Where's Castruchio, her husband?

CARDINAL. He's rode to Naples to take possession
  Of Antonio's citadel.   325

BOSOLA. Believe me, you have done a very happy turn.

CARDINAL. Fail not to come: – there is the master-key
  Of our lodgings; and by that you may conceive
  What trust I plant in you.

BOSOLA.   You shall find me ready.

Exit CARDINAL.

O poor Antonio, though nothing be so needful   330
  To thy estate as pity, yet I find
  Nothing so dangerous. I must look to my footing:
  In such slippery ice-pavements, men had need
  To be frost-nail'd well; they may break their necks else.
  The precedent's here afore me: how this man   335
  Bears up in blood! seems fearless! Why, 'tis well:

Security some men call the suburbs of hell,
Only a dead wall between. Well, good Antonio,
I'll seek thee out, and all my care shall be
To put thee into safety from the reach 340
Of these most cruel biters, that have got
Some of thy blood already. It may be
I'll join with thee, in a most just revenge.
The weakest arm is strong enough, that strikes
With the sword of justice: – still methinks the duchess 345
Haunts me: there, there! –
'Tis nothing but my melancholy.
O Penitence, let me truly taste thy cup,
That throws men down, only to raise them up.

Exit.

Act Five, Scene Three

Enter ANTONIO *and* DELIO. [*There is an*] ECHO *from the Duchess'*
grave.

DELIO. Yon's the cardinal's window: – this fortification
 Grew from the ruins of an ancient abbey;
 And to yon side o' th' river, lies a wall,
 Piece of a cloister, which in my opinion
 Gives the best echo that you ever heard, 5
 So hollow, and so dismal, and withal
 So plain in the distinction of our words,
 That many have suppos'd it is a spirit
 That answers.

ANTONIO. I do love these ancient ruins:
 We never tread upon them but we set 10
 Our foot upon some reverend history.
 And questionless, here in this open court,
 Which now lies naked to the injuries

Of stormy weather, some men lie interr'd
Lov'd the church so well, and gave so largely to 't,   15
They thought it should have canopy'd their bones
Till doomsday; but all things have their end:
Churches and cities, which have diseases like to men,
Must have like death that we have.

ECHO.   *Like death that we have.*

DELIO. Now the echo hath caught you: –

ANTONIO. It groan'd methought, and gave   20
    A very deadly accent.

ECHO.   *Deadly accent.*

DELIO. I told you 'twas a pretty one: you may make it
    A huntsman, or a falconer, a musician,
    Or a thing of sorrow.

ECHO.   *A thing of sorrow.*

ANTONIO. Ay sure: that suits it best.

ECHO.   *That suits it best.*   25

ANTONIO. 'Tis very like my wife's voice.

ECHO.   *Ay, wife's voice.*

DELIO. Come, let's walk farther from 't: –
    I would not have you go to th' cardinal's tonight:
    Do not.

ECHO.   *Do not.*

DELIO. Wisdom doth not more moderate wasting sorrow   30
    Than time: take time for 't; be mindful of thy safety.

ECHO. *Be mindful of thy safety.*

ANTONIO.   Necessity compels me:
    Make scrutiny throughout the passes
    Of your own life, you'll find it impossible
    To fly your fate.

ECHO.   *O, fly your fate!*   35

DELIO. Hark: the dead stones seem to have pity on you
    And give you good counsel.

ANTONIO. Echo, I will not talk with thee,
    For thou art a dead thing.

ECHO.   *Thou art a dead thing.*

ANTONIO. My duchess is asleep now,   40
    And her little ones, I hope sweetly: O heaven,
    Shall I never see her more?

ECHO.   *Never see her more.*

ANTONIO. I mark'd not one repetition of the echo
    But that: and on the sudden, a clear light
    Presented me a face folded in sorrow.   45

DELIO. Your fancy, merely.

ANTONIO. Come: I'll be out of this ague;
    For to live thus is not indeed to live:
    It is a mockery, and abuse of life –
    I will not henceforth save myself by halves;   50
    Lose all, or nothing.

DELIO.   Your own virtue save you!
    I'll fetch your eldest son, and second you:
    It may be that the sight of his own blood
    Spread in so sweet a figure may beget
    The more compassion.

ANTONIO.   How ever, fare you well;   55
    Though in our miseries Fortune have a part,
    Yet in our noble suff'rings she hath none –
    Contempt of pain, that we may call our own.

    Exeunt.

Act Five, Scene Four

Enter CARDINAL, PESCARA, MALATESTE, RODERIGO, *and* GRISOLAN.

CARDINAL. You shall not watch tonight by the sick prince,
  His grace is very well recover'd.

MALATESTE. Good my lord, suffer us.

CARDINAL.   O, by no means;
  The noise, and change of object in his eye,
  Doth more distract him: I pray, all to bed,   5
  And though you hear him in his violent fit,
  Do not rise, I entreat you.

PESCARA. So sir, we shall not –

CARDINAL.   Nay, I must have you promise
  Upon your honours, for I was enjoin'd to 't
  By himself; and he seem'd to urge it sensibly.   10

PESCARA. Let our honours bind this trifle.

CARDINAL. Nor any of your followers.

MALATESTE.   Neither.

CARDINAL. It may be to make trial of your promise
  When he's asleep, myself will rise, and feign
  Some of his mad tricks, and cry out for help,   15
  And feign myself in danger.

MALATESTE.   If your throat were cutting,
  I'd not come at you, now I have protested against it.

CARDINAL. Why, I thank you.

  [*Withdraws.*]

GRISOLAN.   'Twas a foul storm tonight.

RODERIGO. The Lord Ferdinand's chamber shook like an osier.

MALATESTE. 'Twas nothing but pure kindness in the devil   20
  To rock his own child.

Exeunt [all except the CARDINAL].

CARDINAL. The reason why I would not suffer these
    About my brother, is because at midnight
    I may with better privacy convey
    Julia's body to her own lodging: –   25
    O, my conscience!
    I would pray now: but the devil takes away my heart
    For having any confidence in prayer.
    About this hour I appointed Bosola
    To fetch the body: when he hath serv'd my turn,   30
    He dies.

    Exit. Enter BOSOLA.

BOSOLA. Hah? 'twas the cardinal's voice: I heard him name
    Bosola, and my death: listen, I hear one's footing.

    Enter FERDINAND.

FERDINAND. Strangling is a very quiet death.

BOSOLA [*aside*]. Nay then, I see I must stand upon my guard.   35

FERDINAND. What say' to that? whisper, softly: do you agree to 't?
    So it must be done i' th' dark: the cardinal
    Would not for a thousand pounds the doctor should see it.

    Exit.

BOSOLA. My death is plotted; here's the consequence of murder:
    We value not desert, nor Christian breath,   40
    When we know black deeds must be cur'd with death.

    Enter ANTONIO *and* SERVANT.

SERVANT. Here stay sir, and be confident, I pray:
    I'll fetch you a dark lantern.

    Exit.

ANTONIO. Could I take him at his prayers,
    There were hope of pardon.

BOSOLA.   Fall right my sword! [*Stabs him.*]   45
    I'll not give thee so much leisure as to pray.

ANTONIO. O, I am gone! Thou hast ended a long suit
   In a minute.

BOSOLA.   What art thou?

ANTONIO.   A most wretched thing,
   That only have thy benefit in death,
   To appear myself.

   [*Enter* SERVANT *with a light.*]

SERVANT.   Where are you, sir?   50

ANTONIO. Very near my home: – Bosola!

SERVANT.   O, misfortune!

BOSOLA. Smother thy pity, thou art dead else: – Antonio!
   The man I would have sav'd 'bove mine own life!
   We are merely the stars' tennis-balls, struck and banded
   Which way please them – O good Antonio,   55
   I'll whisper one thing in thy dying ear
   Shall make thy heart break quickly: Thy fair duchess
   And two sweet children –

ANTONIO.   Their very names
   Kindle a little life in me.

BOSOLA.   Are murder'd!

ANTONIO. Some men have wish'd to die   60
   At the hearing of sad tidings: I am glad
   That I shall do 't in sadness; I would not now
   Wish my wounds balm'd, nor heal'd, for I have no use
   To put my life to. In all our quest of greatness,
   Like wanton boys whose pastime is their care,   65
   We follow after bubbles, blown in th' air.
   Pleasure of life, what is' t? only the good hours
   Of an ague; merely a preparative to rest,
   To endure vexation: – I do not ask
   The process of my death; only commend me   70
   To Delio.

BOSOLA. Break heart! –

ANTONIO.   And let my son fly the courts of princes.

[*Dies.*]

BOSOLA. Thou seem'st to have lov'd Antonio?

SERVANT.   I brought him hither,
    To have reconcil'd him to the cardinal

BOSOLA. I do not ask thee that: –   75
    Take him up, if thou tender thine own life,
    And bear him, where the Lady Julia
    Was wont to lodge. – O, my fate moves swift!
    I have this cardinal in the forge already,
    Now I'll bring him to th' hammer: – O direful misprision!   80
    I will not imitate things glorious,
    No more than base: I'll be mine own example.
    On, on: and look thou represent, for silence,
    The thing thou bear'st.

    Exeunt.

Act Five Scene Five

Enter CARDINAL, *with a book.*

CARDINAL. I am puzzled in a question about hell:
    He says, in hell there's one material fire,
    And yet it shall not burn all men alike.
    Lay him by: – how tedious is a guilty conscience!
    When I look into the fish-ponds, in my garden,   5
    Methinks I see a thing, arm'd with a rake
    That seems to strike at me: –

Enter BOSOLA, *and* SERVANT *with* ANTONIO's *body.*

                        Now! art thou come?
    Thou look'st ghastly:

There sits in thy face some great determination,
Mix'd with some fear.

BOSOLA.   Thus it lightens into action: 10
I am come to kill thee.

CARDINAL.   Hah? help! our guard!

BOSOLA. Thou art deceiv'd:
They are out of thy howling.

CARDINAL. Hold: and I will faithfully divide
Revenues with thee.

BOSOLA.   Thy prayers and proffers   15
Are both unseasonable.

CARDINAL.   Raise the watch!
We are betray'd!

BOSOLA.   I have confin'd your flight:
I'll suffer your retreat to Julia's chamber,
But no further.

CARDINAL.   Help! we are betray'd!

*Enter[, above,] PESCARA, MALATESTE, RODERIGO [, and
GRISOLAN].*

MALATESTE.   Listen: –   19

CARDINAL. My dukedom for rescue!

RODERIGO.   Fie upon his counterfeiting!

MALATESTE. Why, 'tis not the cardinal.

RODERIGO.   Yes, yes, 'tis he:
But I'll see him hang'd, ere I'll go down to him.

CARDINAL. Here's a plot upon me, I am assaulted! I am lost,
Unless some rescue!

GRISOLAN.   He doth this pretty well:
But it will not serve to laugh me out of mine honour.   25

CARDINAL. The sword's at my throat: –

RODERIGO.   You would not bawl so loud then.

MALATESTE. Come, come:
   Let's go to bed: he told us thus much aforehand.

PESCARA. He wish'd you should not come at him: but believe 't,
   The accent of the voice sounds not in jest.   30
   I'll down to him, howsoever, and with engines
   Force ope the doors. [*Exit above.*]

RODERIGO.   Let's follow him aloof,
   And note how the cardinal will laugh at him.

   [*Exeunt, above,* MALATESTE, RODERIGO, *and* GRISOLAN.]

BOSOLA. There's for you first –

   He kills the Servant.

   'Cause you shall not unbarricade the door   35
   To let in rescue.

CARDINAL. What cause hast thou to pursue my life?

BOSOLA.   Look there: –

CARDINAL. Antonio!

BOSOLA.   Slain by my hand unwittingly: –
   Pray, and be sudden; when thou kill'd'st thy sister,
   Thou took'st from Justice her most equal balance,   40
   And left her naught but her sword.

CARDINAL.   O, mercy!

BOSOLA. Now it seems thy greatness was only outward;
   For thou fall'st faster of thyself, than calamity
   Can drive thee. I'll not waste longer time: there! [*Stabs him.*]   44

CARDINAL. Thou hast hurt me: –

BOSOLA.   Again! [*Stabs him again.*]

CARDINAL.   Shall I die like a leveret
   Without any resistance? help, help, help!
   I am slain!

Enter FERDINAND.

FERDINAND. Th' alarum! give me a fresh horse:
    Rally the vaunt-guard, or the day is lost:
    Yield, yield! I give you the honour of arms,
    Shake my sword over you – will you yield?   50

CARDINAL. Help me, I am your brother.

FERDINAND.   The devil!
    My brother fight upon the adverse party?
    There flies your ransom.

He wounds the CARDINAL, *and in the scuffle gives* BOSOLA
his death-wound.

CARDINAL.   O Justice!
    I suffer now, for what hath former been:
    Sorrow is held the eldest child of sin.   55

FERDINAND. Now you're brave fellows: – Caesar's fortune
    was harder than Pompey's; Caesar died in the arms of
    prosperity, Pompey at the feet of disgrace: – you both died
    in the field. The pain's nothing: pain many times is taken
    away with the apprehension of greater, as the toothache   60
    with the sight of a barber that comes to pull it out – there's
    philosophy for you.

BOSOLA. Now my revenge is perfect:

He kills FERDINAND.

                              sink, thou main cause
    Of my undoing! – The last part of my life
    Hath done me best service.   65

FERDINAND. Give me some wet hay, I am broken-winded –
    I do account this world but a dog-kennel:
    I will vault credit, and affect high pleasures,
    Beyond death.

BOSOLA.   He seems to come to himself,
    Now he's so near the bottom.   70

FERDINAND. My sister! O! my sister! there's the cause on 't:
 Whether we fall by ambition, blood, or lust,
 Like diamonds, we are cut with our own dust. [*Dies.*]

CARDINAL. Thou hast thy payment too.

BOSOLA. Yes, I hold my weary soul in my teeth,   75
 'Tis ready to part from me: – I do glory
 That thou, which stood'st like a huge pyramid
 Begun upon a large and ample base,
 Shalt end in a little point, a kind of nothing.   79

 [*Enter* PESCARA, MALATESTE, RODERIGO, *and*
 GRISOLAN.]

PESCARA. How now, my lord?

MALATESTE.   O, sad disaster!

RODERIGO.   How comes this?

BOSOLA. Revenge, for the Duchess of Malfi, murdered
 By th' Arragonian brethren; for Antonio,
 Slain by this hand; for lustful Julia,
 Poison'd by this man; and lastly, for myself,
 That was an actor in the main of all   85
 Much 'gainst mine own good nature, yet i' th' end
 Neglected.

PESCARA.   How now, my lord?

CARDINAL.   Look to my brother:
 He gave us these large wounds, as we were struggling
 Here i' th' rushes: – and now, I pray, let me
 Be laid by, and never thought of. [*Dies.*]   90

PESCARA. How fatally, it seems, he did withstand
 His own rescue.

MALATESTE.   Thou wretched thing of blood,
 How came Antonio by his death?

BOSOLA. In a mist: I know not how –
 Such a mistake as I have often seen   95

In a play: – O, I am gone! –
We are only like dead walls, or vaulted graves,
That ruin'd, yields no echo: – Fare you well –
It may be pain, but no harm to me to die
In so good a quarrel. O, this gloomy world!   100
In what a shadow, or deep pit of darkness,
Doth womanish and fearful mankind live!
Let worthy minds ne'er stagger in distrust
To suffer death, or shame for what is just –
Mine is another voyage. [*Dies.*]   105

PESCARA. The noble Delio, as I came to th' palace,
    Told me of Antonio's being here, and show'd me
    A pretty gentleman, his son and heir.

Enter DELIO [*with Antonio's* SON].

MALATESTE. O sir, you come too late!

DELIO.   I heard so, and
    Was arm'd for 't ere I came. Let us make noble use   110
    Of this great ruin; and join all our force
    To establish this young, hopeful gentleman
    In's mother's right. These wretched eminent things
    Leave no more fame behind 'em than should one
    Fall in a frost, and leave his print in snow;   115
    As soon as the sun shines, it ever melts,
    Both form, and matter: – I have ever thought
    Nature doth nothing so great, for great men,
    As when she's pleas'd to make them lords of truth:
    Integrity of life is fame's best friend,   120
    Which nobly, beyond death, shall crown the end.

Glossary

Alexander and Lodowick – Two friends who were indistinguishable from each other. Lodowick married in Alexander's name but slept with an unsheathed sword between himself and the woman to avoid compromising her.

angels – coins stamped with angels

apricocks – apricots

arras – a wall hanging

arras (3.2) – a white powder, modern arrowroot

barber – barbers acted as dentists

Barber-Chirugeons' Hall – The Barber-Surgeons, one of the London Guilds, had an anatomical museum

basilisk – a fabulous monster whose breath and sight could kill

bewray – betray

black-guard – kitchen staff

bottom – ship

cabinet – private room

caetera (Latin) – the rest is not examined

careening . . . disembogue – Bosola compares the old lady to a ship that has to have its peeling paint scraped off before it is fit for sea again

Charon – the ferryman in Greek myth who took the dead to Hades across the river Styx

cheat – escheat, a type of tenancy that could be terminated if the tenant committed a crime

chirugeons – surgeons

clew – originally a ball of thread, hence a guide, since thread guides you through a maze

cockatrix – a mythical snake that could kill with a look

cod-piece – a flap or bag at the front of men's breeches

complimental – accomplished

cousin-german – first cousin

coulters – plough shares

cullis – medicinal broth

Danaës – Danaë, in classical mythology, was seduced by Jupiter in the form of a shower of gold

Daphne, Syrinx, Anaxerete – mythological women punished for sleeping with gods

dark lantern – a lantern that can open and close to reveal or hide the light

engines – tools

enginous – ingenious

fathingales – a type of petticoat

fetch a frisk – cut a caper

figure – horoscope

frost-nail'd – wearing well studded footwear

Gordian – the Gordian knot was impossible to untie; Alexander the Great cut it with a sword

Grecian horse – the Trojan Horse

guarded sumpter cloth – decorated saddle cloth

Helvetian translation – Bible published in Switzerland

humorous – bad tempered

imposthume – abscess

intelligence/r – spy/ing

jennet – a type of horse

lord of the ascendant – in astrology, ruling planet

luxurious – lustful

mandragora – mandrake, used as a sleeping potion

mandrake – plant with a man-shaped root, associated with madness, supposed to shriek when pulled up

mother – suffocation associated with hysteria

night-cap – term for part of the dress of a lawyer

Paracelsus – 16th-century magician, alchemist, astrologer

Paris – in Greek myth, he was asked to judge the relative beauty of three goddesses; his decision led to the Trojan War

Pasquil's paper bullets – Pasquinades, satirical verses

Pepin – Pippin, a French king, probably Pippin III, the father of Charlemagne

Per verba (Latin) – 'By words about the present'

pies – magpies

pippin ... crab – grow a sweet apple on a crab apple tree

placket – opening in a skirt, with obscene connotations

plastic – modelling

politic – crafty

poniard – dagger

Portia – committed suicide following her husband Brutus's death at the battle of Philippi

presence – the room where a ruler holds formal audiences

Quietus est (Latin) – Discharge, used in accounting to indicate that the records were correct.

quoit the sledge – throw the hammer

radical – answerable

reversion – inheritance

roaring boys – hooligans

salvatory of green mummy – an ointment container filled with decaying material from a mummy

sloughs – swamps

Spanish fig – a term of contempt

spheres – the stars and planets were believed to move in transparent spheres

springal – stripling

strings . . . bands – parts of the dress of a lawyer

Switzer – a Swiss guard

Tantalus – mythological character condemned eternally to reach for food that was just out of reach

tents – in 1.1, a pun on the normal meaning and the sense of wound dressings

tetter – skin disease

took the ring – won the jousting contest

transportation – export

turtle – turtle dove

vaunt-guard – vanguard

Vulcan's engine – in classical myth, the net the god Vulcan used to catch his wife Venus in the arms of Mars

winding sheet – sheet used to wrap a dead body

wolf – the disease lupus